for 11 - 14s

BOOK 1

CHRISTIAN FOCUS PUBLICATIONS

We believe that the Bible is God's word to mankind, and that it contains everything we need to know in order to be reconciled with God and live in a way that is pleasing to him. Therefore, we believe it is vital to teach young teens accurately from the Bible, being careful to teach each passage's true meaning in an appropriate way for the age group, rather than selecting a 'teen's message' from a Biblical passage.

TⁿT Ministries (which stands for Teaching and Training Ministries) was launched in February 1993 by Christians from a broad variety of denominational backgrounds who were concerned that teaching the Bible to children be taken seriously. The leaders were in charge of the Sunday School of 50 teachers at St Helen's Bishopsgate, an evangelical church in the City of London, for 13 years, during which time a range of Biblical teaching materials was developed. TⁿT Ministries also runs training days for Sunday School teachers.

CONTENTS

On the Way for 11-14s / Book 1

Contributors

Preparation of Bible material:
Wendy Barber
Thalia Blundell

Editing:
David Jackman

Activities & Puzzles:
Wendy Barber
Emma Blundell
Thalia Blundell
Rachel Garforth-Bles
Jennefer Lord
Mick Margesson

On The Way for 11-14s works on a 3 year syllabus consisting of 6 books. It builds on the 9-11s syllabus and introduces young teens to study the Bible in a way which is challenging and intellectually stretching. Because they are often unprepared to take things at face value and are encouraged to question everything, it is important to satisfy the mind while touching the heart. Therefore, some of the lessons are designed to introduce the idea of further Bible study skills, e.g. the use of a concordance, a character study, studying a single verse or a passage.

Lessons are grouped in series, each of which is introduced by a series overview stating the aims of the series, the lesson aim for each week, and an appropriate memory verse. Every lesson, in addition to an aim, has study notes to enable the teacher to understand the Bible passage, a suggestion to focus attention on the study to follow, a question section and an activity for the group to do. The question section consists of 2-3 questions designed to help in discussing the application of the Bible passage. The course can be joined at any time during its 3 year cycle.

To prepare a Sunday School lesson properly takes at least one evening (2-3 hours). It is helpful to read the Bible passage several days before teaching it to allow time to mull over what it is saying.

When preparing a lesson the following steps should be taken -

1. PRAY!

In a busy world this is very easy to forget. We are unable to understand God's word without his help and we need to remind ourselves of that fact before we start.

2. READ THE BIBLE PASSAGE

This should be done *before* reading the lesson manual. Our resource is the Bible, not what someone says about it. The Bible study notes in the lesson manual are a commentary on the passage to help you understand it.

3. LOOK AT THE LESSON AIM

This should reflect the main teaching of the passage. Plan how that can be packaged appropriately for the age group you teach.

4. TEACHING THE BIBLE PASSAGE

This should take place in the context of simple Bible study. Do ensure that the children use the same version of the Bible. Prior to the lesson decide how the passage will be read, (e.g. one verse at a time), and who should do the reading. Is the passage short enough to read the whole of it or should some parts be paraphrased by the teacher? Work through the passage, deciding which points should be raised. Design simple questions to bring out the main teaching of the passage. The first questions should elicit the facts and should be designed so that they cannot be answered by a simple 'no' or 'yes'. If a group member reads out a Bible verse as the answer, praise him/her and then ask ask him/her to put it in his/her own words. Once the facts have been established go on to application questions, encouraging the group to think through how the teaching can be applied to their lives. The question section is designed to help you when it comes to discussing the application of the Bible passage.

5. VISUAL AIDS

Pictures are very rarely required for this age group. A Bible Timeline is useful so that the young people can see where the Bible passage they are studying comes in the big picture of God's revelation to his people. You can find one at the back of this book. A map is helpful to demonstrate distances, etc. A flip chart or similar is handy to summarise the lesson.

6. ACTIVITIES AND PUZZLES

These are designed to reinforce the Bible teaching and very little prior preparation (if any) is required by the teacher.

BENEFITS OF ON THE WAY

- Encourages the leaders to study the Bible for themselves.

- Teaches young people Bible-study skills.

- Everything you need is in the one book, so there is no need to buy activity books.

- Undated materials allow you to use the lessons to fit your situation without wasting materials.

- Once you have the entire syllabus, there is no need to repurchase.

On The Way for 11-14s is designed to teach young teens how to read and understand a passage of Scripture and then apply it to their lives (see How to Prepare a Lesson). Before learning how to study the Bible they need to know what it is and how to find their way around it.

The Bible

Christians believe that the Bible is God's word and contains all we need to know in order to live in relationship with God and with each other. It is the way God has chosen to reveal himself to mankind; it not only records historical facts but also interprets those facts. It is not a scientific text book.

What does the Bible consist of?

The Bible is God's story. It is divided into 2 sections - the Old and New Testaments. 'Testament' means 'covenant' or 'promise'.

The Old Testament contains 39 books covering the period from creation to about 400 years before the birth of Jesus. It records God's mighty acts of creation, judgment and mercy as well as their interpretation through the words of the prophets.

The New Testament is made up of 27 books containing details of the life, death and resurrection of Jesus, the spread of the gospel in the early Church, Christian doctrine and the final judgment.

Who wrote the Bible?

The books of the Bible were written by many different people, some known and others not. Christians believe that all these authors were inspired by God (2 Peter 1:20-21, 2 Timothy 3:16). As a result we can trust what it says.

How can we find our way around it?

Each book in the Bible is divided into chapters, each one of which contains a number of verses. When the Books were written originally the chapter and verse divisions were absent. These have been added to enable the readers to find their way around. When written down they are recorded in the following way, Genesis 5:1-10. This tells us to look up the book of Genesis, chapter 5, verses 1 to 10.

At the front of the Bible is a contents page, listing the books in the order in which they come in the Bible. It is perfectly acceptable to look up the index to see which page to turn to.

Aids to teach the Bible passage

- Many of the lessons have activity pages that help to bring out the main teaching of the Bible passage.
- Packs of maps and charts can be purchased from Christian book shops.
- A Bible Time Line is useful to reinforce the chronology of the Bible (see back of this book).

Questions to aid in understanding

Periodically use the following questions to help the young people understand the passage:
- Who wrote it?
- To whom was it written?
- When was it written?
- What situation is being described? (if applicable)

THE BIBLE LIBRARY

To make a chart of the Bible Library enlarge the template below and photocopy as required. Draw 2 sets of shelves on a large piece of paper (see diagram). Label the shelves. Cut off the unwanted books from each set and write the names of the books on the spines. Glue the books onto the appropriate shelves in the order in which they appear in the Bible.

The Bible Library

Old Testament	New Testament
Law (5 books)	Gospels & Acts (5)
History (12 books)	Paul's Epistles (13)
Poetry & Wisdom (5)	Other Epistles (8)
Prophets (17 books)	Prophecy (1 book)

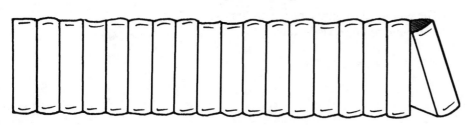

OVERVIEW
Abraham

Week 1 | **The Call** — Hebrews 11:8-19, Genesis 11:27 - 12:20
To introduce Abraham and to discover that his faith in God was demonstrated by obedience.

Week 2 | **The Choice** — Genesis 13:1-18
To teach the importance of making right choices.

Week 3 | **The Covenant** — Genesis 15:1-21; 17:1-27
To learn about God's covenant with Abraham.

Week 4 | **The Consequences of Unbelief** — Genesis 16:1-15
To demonstrate the consequences of unbelief.

Week 5 | **The Promise Fulfilled** — Genesis 18:1-15; 21:1-21
To learn that God can be trusted to keep his promises.

Week 6 | **The Test** — Genesis 22:1-19
To learn that God requires us to put him first.

Week 7 | **The Way Forward** — Genesis 24:1-67
To learn that God guides those who obey him.

SERIES AIMS

1. To discover that Abraham was a man like us, with human failings, and to see what it was that caused him to be called the friend of God.

2. To learn how to apply what we learn about Abraham to our own lives.

MEMORY WORK

Let us hold unswervingly to the hope we profess, for he who promised is faithful.

Hebrews 10:23

Abraham, Friend of God

The book of Genesis splits into 11 sections, each one apart from the first beginning with the words, 'This is the account of .....' (2:4; 5:1; 6:9; 10:1; 11:10; 11:27; 25:12; 25:19; 36:1; 37:2). The final 5 sections deal with the family of Abraham and the first 2 series in this book look at the establishment of God's covenant with Abraham and his descendants. The lessons are split into 2 sections, weeks 1-7 dealing primarily with Abraham and weeks 8-14 with the life of Jacob. The last section (the life of Joseph) will be studied in Book 3.

Abraham, originally called Abram, was descended from Noah's son, Shem, and was the son of Terah (Genesis 11:10-26). He was born in Ur in Babylonia and, together with his wife, Sarai (later to be called Sarah), and nephew, Lot, was taken to Haran by his father Terah (Genesis 11:27-31). After Terah died God called Abram to leave his country, relatives and home and go to the land which God would show him (Genesis 12:1). Abram was now 75 years old and taking Sarai, with Lot, he did as God commanded, eventually settling in Canaan. Abram became a nomad, living in tents, and he moved around Canaan, first settling in one place, then in another.

Abram became very wealthy (Genesis 12:16; 13:2), but had no son to succeed him. When God called Abram to leave Haran he promised him that he would become a great nation (Genesis 12:2). This promise was repeated following Abram and Lot's separation (Genesis 13:14-17), and when God made a formal covenant with Abram (Genesis 15:4-6). After 10 years had passed Abram still had no son, so he and Sarai decide to help the matter along by Abram taking Sarai's maid, Hagar, as a concubine (Genesis 16:1-3). Ishmael was born as a result and Abram had an heir (Genesis 16:15). However, Ishmael was not the heir whom God had chosen, and God repeated his promise of a son by Sarai to Abram when he was 99 years old (Genesis 17:1-22). It was at that stage that Abram's name was changed to Abraham - father of a multitude. The promised son, Isaac, was born when Abraham was 100 years old and Sarah was 90 (Genesis 21:1-2).

While Isaac was still a boy, God tested Abraham's faith by commanding him to sacrifice Isaac. Abraham set out to obey God, even though Isaac was the one through whom God had promised Abraham's descendants would come. At the last moment, God called out to Abraham and stopped him killing Isaac. God provided a ram to be sacrificed in Isaac's place and then reaffirmed his covenant with Abraham and his descendants (Genesis 22:1-18).

Abraham died aged 175 years. Through Isaac, he became the father of the Jews (Genesis 17:19, Romans 4:1) and through Ishmael, the father of the Arabs (Genesis 17:20; 25:12-18). He is revered by Jews, Christians, and Muslims. His life was summarised by Stephen in Acts 7:2-8 and his faith summarised in Hebrews 11:8-19. He is recorded as being the friend of God in 2 Chronicles 20:7, and it is by faith that God accepted him as righteous (Romans 4:3, Genesis 15:6). Abraham's faith in God was demonstrated by his obedience to God's word (Hebrews 11:8,11,17).

As we study Abraham's life we will discover that he was a normal man, who succumbed to temptation like we all do, yet he was called the friend of God.

PREPARATION

Hebrews 11:8-19, Genesis 11:27 - 12:20

LESSON AIMS

To introduce Abraham and to discover that his faith in God was demonstrated by obedience.

God's call to Abraham was not on the grounds of any religious or spiritual merit of Abraham's, but purely in accordance with God's choice. Joshua later confirmed that Terah and his family - descendants of Shem - shared in the idolatry around them (Joshua 24:2), but it seems clear that this idolatry did not have the grosser elements that had so poisoned Canaanite religion, e.g. child sacrifice. Without God's call Abraham would not have known God.

Therefore, the call to leave his father's household and country would preserve Abraham from the pagan influence of home and family. Whilst Abraham was being called to a country in which the loss of the knowledge of God had led to even greater depravity of morals and religion, it may have been less of a threat than the shallow, yet deceptive religiosity of his family. Nevertheless, Abraham recognised the potential of local culture to corrupt by insisting that Isaac's wife came from his relatives, not from amongst the local women (Genesis 24:1-4).

Hebrews

11:8   Abraham's faith was demonstrated by obedience.

11:10   See Revelation 21:1-27.

11:11   Abraham believed God would keep his promises.

11:17   Another example of Abraham's obedience. We need to recognise that it was not the amount of faith that was important, but rather the fact of Abraham's faith being placed in a great big God.

Genesis

For location of place names and route of Abraham's journey, please refer to pages 10 and 11.

For NT commentaries on this passage see Acts 7:2-7 and Hebrews 11:8-10.

11:27   It would be helpful to make a family tree that can be added to as the weeks go by.

11:31   'Terah took his son ....'. Acts 7:3 seems to suggest that it was Abraham who was called. There is no reason to suppose that both may not be true. The first stage may have been taken unconsciously in response to God's call. Alternatively, v.31 is the scene as it appeared to the world. The reality of it was God's call (Acts 7:2-3). For whatever reason the journey was interrupted until the death of his father, when Abram was free to continue his journey in response to God's call.

11:32   Terah's age at death presents a difficulty. Various explanations have been suggested. It may be that Abram was the youngest son, being mentioned first in v.26 because of his importance. Or it may be that Terah's age was 145, as given in an alternative reading of the text (Samaritan Pentateuch).

12:1-3   The call may have taken place in Ur ('**had said**' v.1), making this a reminder of the original call, prompting Abram to resume his journey in v.4.

   God's promise to Abram:
   v.1 Go to the land I will show you.
   v.2 Many descendants
   w.2-3   Abram will be a blessing (See Galatians 3:6-9).

12:2-3   God's blessing means his gracious giving to one in need, material and spiritual. In the wider sense, God's blessing to mankind will be the reversal of the curse of God in Genesis 3:14-19. Therefore, those who reject the blessing through Abraham reject God.

12:4   Note Abram's response.

12:7   God fulfils the promise (cf. 12:1).

12:10　Having been told by God that he was in the right land, Abram leaves the land due to adverse circumstances.

12:11-13　Does Abram demonstrate trust in God in these verses? (Look back to the promise in 12:2 - God had not yet fulfilled this promise.)

12:14-16　It all turned out as Abram had predicted. He may have thought how sensible he had been as the wealth poured in ......

12:17　**but** God took a hand.

1. How does Abram demonstrate his faith in God? Give specific examples.

2. Why did Abram fall into temptation so soon after God had fulfilled part of his promise to him? (12:10-13). Can this help us to avoid succumbing to temptation?

3. What sort of witness was Abram to Pharaoh? (12:14-19).

Following Instructions
Photocopy the instruction sheet on page 11 and distribute to every member of the group. Make sure that everyone has a pen. Tell them that they have a maximum of 5 minutes to complete the instuctions on the sheet. Make sure that there is a reward for any who complete the task successfully. At the end of the exercise discuss the importance of listening to and following instructions. Let's see what Abraham did when God gave him some instructions that did not make much sense to him at the time.

Map to show Abram's journey (see page 10).

Divide the group into teams and use a quiz to review the Bible passage.

On page 11 is a representational drawing of Abram's journey from Ur to Haran and then from Haran to Canaan. Redraw it to the scale you will be using in your situation, i.e. on a large sheet of paper on a board in front of the group, or to fit on the desk or table where they are sitting.

The aim is to get Abram from Ur to Canaan and the first team to do this wins. There are 6 steps between Ur and Canaan, indicated on the diagram by arrows. In order to move from step to step the team has to acquire an arrow by answering a question correctly.

Requirements:
Representational drawing - 1 for each team.

Eight rectangular cards - a set for each team. On one side the cards are numbered 1 to 8. On the other side of 6 of them there is an arrow (to point the direction of the journey), the remaining 2 cards being left blank. This is to allow for an element of luck in acquiring arrows, so that anyone answering a question incorrectly will not place their team in an irretrievable position.

The cards are placed numbered side up to one side of each team's drawing. Because the journey is longer from Ur to Haran you might want to use 4 arrows to get to Haran and only 2 to complete the journey to Canaan.

Rules:
A question is put to each team in turn and, if answered correctly, one of the team members chooses a card by calling out its number. The card is turned over and if it has an arrow on it is placed in position. If there is no arrow the card is placed to one side.

If an incorrect answer is given the question is put to the other team. If the other team gets it right they choose a card (which again could have an arrow or be blank).

Allow 10-15 minutes for the quiz. This should mean that each team will have at least 5-6 cards to their credit! Prepare a minimum of 8 questions per team from the Bible passage.

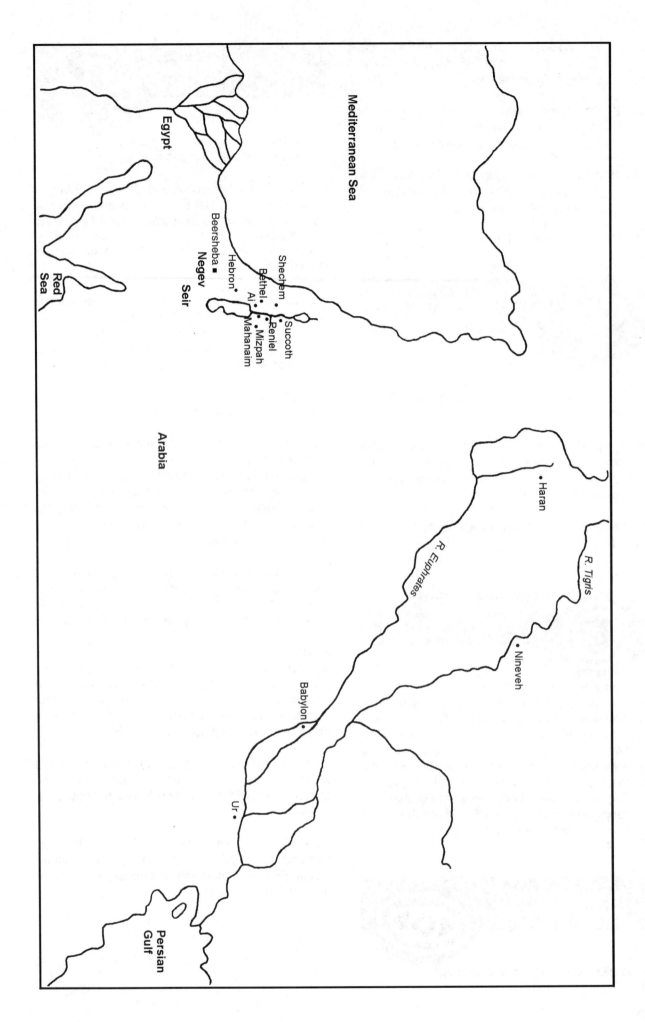

Mediterranean Sea

Egypt

Red
Sea

Beersheba

Negev

Seir

Hebron

Shechem

Bethel

Ai

Mahanaim

Mizpah

Peniel

Succoth

Arabia

Haran

R. Euphrates

R. Tigris

Nineveh

Babylon

Ur

Persian
Gulf

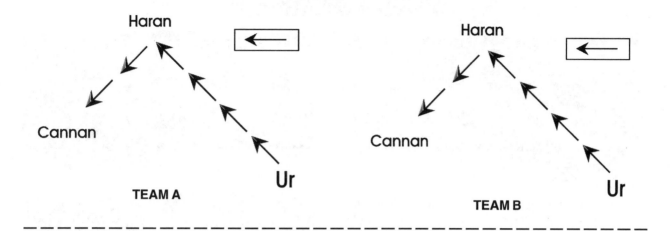

TEAM A

TEAM B

Following Instructions

Follow the instructions on this sheet for a reward.

1. Read all the instructions through before you begin.

2. Write your name in the top right hand corner of this instruction sheet.

3. Tear off a bit of the bottom left corner of this instruction sheet.

4. Do an impression of a cow.

5. Scrumple up this instruction sheet and then open it out again.

6. Hop to one wall of the room and back again.

7. Repeat instruction 4.

8. Draw a circle around the word 'instruction' every time it appears on this sheet.

9. Clap three times as loudly as you can.

10. Do an impression of a dog.

11. Fold this sheet in half with the writing on the outside.

12. Read instruction 13 and say as loudly as you can, 'I am very, very silly.'

13. Ignore instructions 2 to 12, wait a few minutes and then trade this unblemished instruction sheet in for a reward.

PREPARATION

Genesis 13:1-18

LESSON AIMS

To teach the importance of making right choices.

Genesis

13:1   Lot had decided to join Abram when he left Haran for Canaan. Subsequently, he had travelled with Abram to Egypt where he had seen the fertile valleys (v.10).

13:2   Abram was extremely wealthy (see 12:6). He was a person who was respected by others and who had a military force to protect his people and possessions (14:14).

13:3   cf. 12:8.

13:6   Even though Abram was rich, resources were limited, e.g. grass. Perhaps they competed also with the Canaanites and the Perizzites (v.7).

13:8-9   Abram, who had been willing to leave his family in Haran to follow God's call, was now willing to trust that God would guide him. He gave the choice of deciding where to settle to his nephew Lot.

13:10-11   Lot looked at outward things. The land looked wonderful but in reality it was not. In fact, the people of the cities were extremely evil and lawless. Lot wanted the fertile land. He is called righteous Lot in 2 Peter 2:7 - distressed by what he saw in Sodom and Gomorrah.

13:14-17   After Lot had parted from him, God spoke to Abram and renewed his covenant promise. Even though Lot had chosen the Jordan plain, God promised Abram every bit of land that he could see.

13:18   The Oaks of Mamre are 20 miles south of Bethel.

QUESTIONS

1. What does this passage teach about Abram's dependence on God? (13:4; 13:8-9).

2. What criteria did Lot use when making his choice? (13:10-13).

3. What criteria should we use when making a major choice? E.g. knowledge of God and his word, understanding of the situation, knowledge of moral absolutes, possible consequences, peer group pressure.

FOCUS ACTIVITY

The Taste Test. Buy 2 litre bottles of 4 different brands of Cola (or other soft drink). Remove all labelling and rename them 'A', 'B', 'C' and 'D'. Ask each member of the group to taste the different drinks and guess which is which, writing their answers in a grid similar to the one below. Once everyone has made their choices, reveal the correct answers. Discuss what information they used to make their choices. Let's look at the Bible to see what Abraham and Lot did when faced with making a choice.

Bottle	Virgin Cola	Coca Cola	Diet Cola	Asda Cola
A				
B				
C				
D				

Photocopy the activity below for each person with the answers covered. Once the sheets have been completed read out the answers so that the group members can mark their own sheets.

The Choice   Genesis 13:1-18

This activity is designed to show the importance of knowing God and his word in making right choices. Each question has a choice of 3 answers. Go through the questions, ticking your choice of answer. After the sheet has been marked add up your points for your final score.

                                                                      a   b   c

1. Lot was - a) Abram's son, b) Terah's son, c) Haran's son   ☐   ☐   ☐

2. Who was very wealthy? - a) Lot, b) Abram, c) both   ☐   ☐   ☐

3. Lot and Abram decided to part when living at - a) the Negev,   ☐   ☐   ☐
   b) Bethel, c) Shechem

4. Lot's household and Abram's quarrelled about - a) pasture,   ☐   ☐   ☐
   b) money, c) travelling around

5. Who suggested that they part? - a) Lot, b) Abram, c) the   ☐   ☐   ☐
   herdsmen

6. Lot chose to settle where he did because - a) the land was   ☐   ☐   ☐
   fertile, b) the cities were wealthy, c) the land was well watered

7. The people of the cities were - a) wicked, b) not particularly   ☐   ☐   ☐
   wicked, c) good

8. God promised Abram that his descendants would be as
   numerous as - a) the stars in the sky, b) the sand on the sea   ☐   ☐   ☐
   shore, c) the dust of the earth

If you have scored the following points your knowledge of this passage in the Bible is -

       average   13 - 16
       good   17 - 20
       very good 21 - 24

Answers:	1. a)1 b)1 c)3	2. a)2 b)2 c)3	3. a)1 b)3 c)1	4. a)3 b)1 c)1	5. a)1 b)3 c)1
	6. a)2 b)1 c)3	7. a)3 b)1 c)1	8. a)2 b)2 c)3		

PREPARATION

Genesis
15:1-21; 17:1-27

LESSON AIMS

To learn about God's covenant with Abraham.

In these passages, God's covenant or agreement with Abraham is confirmed. God had previously spoken several times to Abraham, outlining the special relationship that God had initiated and the blessings that would follow. Now God identifies himself more fully and sets out the nature of the covenant.

A covenant was a contract between 2 parties where each party was bonded together in a formal relationship. The covenant sets out what is required from each party and what will happen if the covenant is broken. In OT times there were 2 types of covenant or treaty -

1. A suzerainty or vassal covenant was one between an overlord (or great king) and a subject person or nation.

2. A parity covenant was one between equals, e.g. David and Jonathan (1 Samuel 20:12-17,42).

All covenants had a covenant form which consisted of the following:

1. The historical situation.
2. The requirements/stipulations.
3. The response, i.e. what will happen as a result.
4. The witnesses. In covenants between God and his people the witnesses were often heaven and earth. Each OT covenant also had its own special sign, e.g. the rainbow, circumcision.
5. The blessings that would occur if the covenant was kept.
6. The curses - what would happen if the covenant was broken.
7. Public ratification. This usually incorporated a sacrificial meal.
8. Periodic renewal.

15:1 The surrounding tribes were powerful. In Genesis 14:1-24 Lot got caught up in a tribal war and was captured along with all his possessions. When Abram was told about it he took the 318 trained men born in his household and rescued Lot. He routed the 4 kings and their armies and brought back Lot, all his possessions and the people, and possessions of Sodom and Gomorrah. Now God appears to Abram to reassure him of God's protection.

15:2-3 Abram reminded God that he still had no heir (cf. God's promise in 12:2 and 13:15-16).

15:4-6 God renewed his promise of a son. Abram believed God in spite of his age (12:4) and Sarai's barrenness (11:30).

15:7 God reminded Abram of another promise he had made, which had started to come true (cf. 12:1).

15:8 Abram asked for reassurance.

15:10 'cut in two' - this was an oath ritual which was customary in treaty ratification. It symbolised what would happen to the person who broke the treaty.

15:13-16 God told Abram what would happen in the future.

15:17 The smoking brazier and the flaming torch symbolised God's presence (cf. Exodus 3:1-6; 13:21; 19:18).

17:1 Abram is now 99 years old. 24 years have passed since Abram first came to Canaan and 13 since the birth of Ishmael. (The latter will be studied next week.)

17:5 Abraham means 'father of many'.

The covenant form

17:6-8 The historical situation (see also 15:4-6).

17:9-10 The requirements/stipulations.

17:17 The response.

15:5, 13:16 The witnesses - the stars (heaven) and the dust (earth).

17:16 The blessings - a son. Abraham would receive a blessing in the form of Isaac but he would also become a blessing (18:18; 12:3).

15:10,17 The curses are implied - division and war. Sin, the breaking of the covenant, results in separation from God. This is a good opportunity to point out the need for Jesus' death if man was to be reconciled to God.

15:9-21 Public ratification by way of a sacrificial meal. Breaking bread and drinking wine was the normal OT covenant meal. Compare with the Last Supper as a type of NT covenant meal.

22:15-19 Renewal of the covenant. This also took place at the giving of the Law on Mount Sinai.

An outline of the historical fulfilment of the covenant.

	PROMISE	FULFILMENT
17:5	Abraham's new name means 'Father of many nations'	People of many nations throughout the world have become children of Abraham (Galatians 3:29).
17:6	Kings will come from you	The kings of Israel and Judah. The king of kings (Christ himself).
17:7	An everlasting covenant	Fulfilled in the Lord Jesus, God's own son, coming to establish a way for all to be a child of God through faith.
17:8	The land of Canaan will belong to his descendants.	This found its fulfilment in the time of Joshua.
17:9	God chooses a people for himself.	The children of Abraham were God's chosen people.
17:16	God promises Abraham a son with Sarah.	Isaac is born a year later.

1. Abram reminded God of his promise (cf. 15:2 with 12:1-3). Does God ever forget his promises? Is it right to remind him of them?

2. Abram put his trust in God and was declared righteous (15:6). What about the times when Abram didn't trust God, e.g. in Egypt (12:10-20)?

3. Abram still has doubts (15:8). Doubts are obviously not a hindrance to being accepted by God. Why do we doubt? What should we do about our doubts?

Promises, Promises. Every member of the group has to make a promise to do something specific and beneficial for somebody else in the group by the end of today's session. Ask everyone to write their promise on a piece of paper, stating who they are, what they are going to do and who for. Collect up the pieces of paper and tell the group that, at the end of the session, you will read out their promises and find out if they have kept them. Let's look at the Bible to see what promises God made to Abraham.

Remember to read out their promises at the end of the session.

The covenant form as applied to God's covenant with Abraham could be done as a joint class activity.

For the puzzle, photocopy page 17 for each member of the group.

God told Abraham that his descendants would be as numerous as the stars in the sky (Genesis 15:5). Start at the arrow and trace the memory verse through the stars. You can only move between stars that are connected with a straight line. Use every star, but no letter may be used more than once. Add arrows to the lines so that you can retrace your journey if necessary.

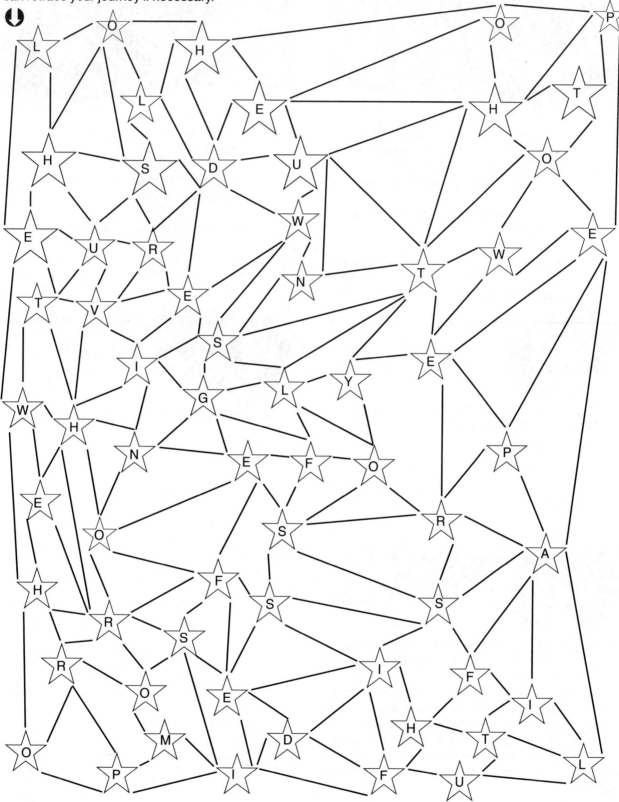

Verse :

Hebrews 10:23

17

PREPARATION

Genesis 16:1-15

16:1-2   God had promised Abram a son - but nothing had happened. Sarai used human wisdom to try and bring about what God had promised. Abram agreed to do as she said.

16:3   10 years had passed since God first made the promise.

16:5   Note the breakdown in relationship between Sarai and Abram. Going against God's law **always** has consequences (cf. 12:10-20).

LESSON AIMS

To demonstrate the consequences of unbelief.

16:6   Abram hands over the responsibility for Hagar's welfare to Sarai.

16:10   Cf. God's promise to Hagar with God's promise to Abram in 13:16.

16:11   Ishmael means 'God hears'.

16:12   Ishmael was the father of the Arabs. See the fulfilment of this prophecy in 25:12-18.

QUESTIONS

1. How does 16:1-3 tie in with 15:6? Why did Abram agree to Sarai's proposition?
2. What were the consequences of Abram's actions:
   - for himself?   - for Sarai?   - for Hagar?
3. If God is a God of forgiveness why doesn't he remove the consequences of wrong actions?

ACTIVITY

Photocopy page 20 for each member of the group.

FOCUS ACTIVITY

Consequences. Photocopy page 19 and give each group member a copy. Each person fills in the blank in the top section and folds that section behind so that it cannot be seen. Each sheet of paper is then passed to the next person, who fills in the second section (which is now the top section). Again, this section is folded over so that it cannot be seen and the sheet is passed on. Repeat this process until the whole sheet has been filled in. Collect in the sheets, unfold them and read them out.

Let's look at the Bible to see what consequences there were for Abram and Sarai.

Consequences

‒‒‒

Once upon a time, somebody called ....

‒‒‒

met up with three friends called ...., ... and

....

‒‒‒

They decided to start ....

‒‒‒

For a time everything went fine, but what they hadn't remembered was

....

‒‒‒

And the consequence was ....

‒‒‒

God had promised Abram a son - but 10 years had passed and nothing had happened. Then Sarai had a bright idea and tried to help God out. To discover the consequence find the 14 words listed at the side of the word square. Each word reads in a straight line horizontally, vertically or diagonally. No letter is used more than once.

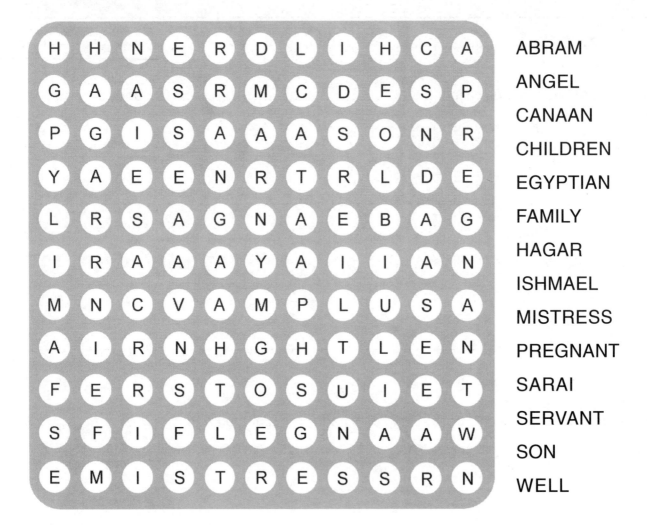

H H N E R D L I H C A	ABRAM
G A A S R M C D E S P	ANGEL
P G I S A A A S O N R	CANAAN
Y A E E N R T R L D E	CHILDREN
L R S A G N A E B A G	EGYPTIAN
I R A A A Y A I I A N	FAMILY
M N C V A M P L U S A	HAGAR
A I R N H G H T L E N	ISHMAEL
F E R S T O S U I E T	MISTRESS
S F I F L E G N A A W	PREGNANT
E M I S T R E S S R N	SARAI
	SERVANT
	SON
	WELL

Now, starting from the top and reading from left to right, write down the remaining letters to discover the consequence of Sarai's bright idea.

PREPARATION

Genesis 18:1-15; 21:1-21

LESSON AIMS

To learn that God can be trusted to keep his promises.

18:1   We are told that the Lord appeared to Abraham. The following verses explain how that happened.

18:2   The impression is of a sudden appearance of the three. This is generally thought to be the Lord and 2 angels.

18:6-8   The meal Abraham gave them was fit for a king, which was very appropriate. He stood by and watched them eat until they had finished, which is a common Bedouin custom.

18:10   A confirmation of the promise of 17:16. (This visitation came very soon after the one in chapter 17, probably within a couple of months.) Now Sarah is included (she can hear all that is going on from the door of the tent).

18:12-14   Although Sarah spoke to herself, God knew what was in her heart. He challenged it with, 'is anything too hard for the Lord?' It reads as if Sarah knew about the promise (Abraham possibly told her after 17:16) and did not believe, as God rebuked her for her unbelief.

18:15   She was then fearful and denied laughing, but was challenged again with the words, 'Yes, you did laugh.' In Hebrews 11:11 she is still seen as a woman of faith.

Note that in an act of worship 'he fell face down'. Abraham also laughed (17:17), though more in amazement than unbelief. Not inappropriately, Isaac means 'he laughs'.

21:5   14 years after Ishmael had been born to Abraham through Hagar (16:16), God fulfilled his promise to Abraham and Sarah and a son was born to them.

21:6   God's promise revealed in chapter 12 is now

fulfilled - and Sarah who laughed in a cynical way is now laughing with true joy and thanking God for his great gift.

21:8   'Weaned' - probably when Isaac was about 2 or 3 years old. So Ishmael may have been in his late teens by this stage.

21:9   'Mocking' - before Isaac's birth Ishmael was probably seen as Abraham's natural heir. To Ishmael, therefore, the celebration of an untimely birth to an aged woman must have seemed particularly distasteful as it marked the end of his personal interest in the inheritance, but it also showed an inability to recognise the work of God. It was, therefore, also scornful of God (see also 16:12 and Galatians 4:28-29).

21:10   See also 16:2-9. Hagar's status was always that of a slave, Sarah's maid. Sarah had total control. Ishmael was entitled to a share of the inheritance but Sarah was determined he would have no part of it. Sarah could not forget Hagar's earlier derision (16:4). She probably also saw Ishmael as a continuing threat (v.10). Did she fully believe God's promises?

21:11   Sarah's distress was equalled by that of Abraham. Isaac was the true heir through whom God would maintain the covenant he had made with Abraham. Yet Ishmael had been his first son, from his 'own body' (15:4). There is no doubt that Ishmael was precious to Abraham (see 17:18) but he was not the son of the promise. In response to Abraham's prayer (17:20) God would bless Ishmael and he would thus enjoy the benefits of God's providential care for all of Abraham's family (v.13).

21:12   God recognised Sarah's responsibility to bring up Isaac in the way she knew best without threat. The atmosphere of hostility would most likely have poisoned relationships and served no one's benefit. God does not condone Sarah's attitude but he recognises and works through people's weaknesses.

21:13   God reinforced the promise he had earlier given to Abraham about Ishmael that He would bless him (17:20).

21:14   When told by God to send them away Abraham obeyed and did it promptly ('early'). Abraham was prepared to trust God to look after Ishmael even though the circumstances did not look very hopeful. Almost a foreshadowing of the later event in which he was prepared to give up Isaac.

        Beersheba - refer to the map on page 10.

21:15-19 At last Hagar could not help Ishmael any more and sat him under a tree, ready to die. She and the boy cried. God gave them water - a well miraculously appeared. So God's promises stand (16:12; 17:20; 21:13). Note also that Ishmael is almost the same spelling in Hebrew as 'God heard' (see 16:11).

21:20-21 The natural affinities of Hagar and Ishmael are emerging, perhaps confirming the wisdom of the parting. His marriage to an Egyptian and his nomadic roving emphasise the separation of the Ishmaelites from the Abrahamic covenant.

NB We see here man's situation and God's grace. Ishmael has no home, food or water and cries to God in despair. God provided a well, displaying his continuing care and blessing - not just a cup of water.

The Desert of Paran was a wilderness situated in the east central region of the Sinai peninsula, north-east from the traditional Sinai.

FOCUS ACTIVITY

Trust the Adverts? Get the group to go through a pile of old magazines and newspapers and cut out all of the advertisments they can find. Once they have collected a large pile get them to look through the adverts and try to work out what promises they are making. E.g.

    1. wear these clothes and you will be successful at work.

    2. use this deodorant and you will be attractive to the opposite sex.

    3. buy this toothpaste and you'll live happily ever after.

You might want to write down the answers on a flip chart or OHP. Finish by asking, 'Do you trust the advertisers to keep their promise?'

You could do the same exercise by showing a video of pre-recorded television adverts.

Point out that we are bombarded with promises all of the time. The important question to ask is whether the person making the promise is trustworthy. Remind them of the promises God made to Abram. Let's look at the Bible to see how these promises were kept.

ACTIVITY

For crossword puzzle photocopy page 23 for each member of the group.

QUESTIONS

1. Abraham discovered that God kept his promises. How can we know whether a person can be trusted to keep their promise?

2. God speaks to Abraham several times in these verses. How can I know when God is speaking to me?

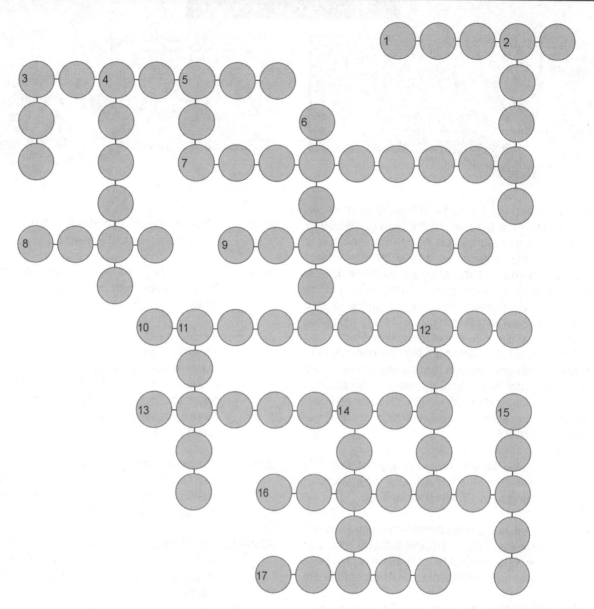

Down

2. The name of the desert Ishmael lived in. (21:21)

3. The one who heard Hagar's cry. (21:17)

4. God promised to make Abraham a great ......

5. What Hagar began to do when they ran out of water. (21:16)

6. What Hagar's son became. (21:20)

11. The name of Sarah's son.

12. The name of Abraham's wife.

14. How many men appeared to Abraham? (18:2)

15. The name of the trees where Abraham lived. (18:1)

Across

1. Where did Ishmael's wife come from? (21:21)

3. The book of the Bible we are studying.

7. The desert Hagar and her son were sent to. (21:14)

8. What Hagar was given by Abraham. (21:14)

9. The name of Hagar's son.

10. Another word for being very upset. (21:11)

13. What God brought to Sarah in her old age. (21:6)

16. To whom did God appear? (18:1)

17. What Sarah baked. (18:6)

PREPARATION

Genesis 22:1-19

LESSON AIMS

To learn that God requires us to put him first.

Isaac has been born in fulfilment of God's promise. Hagar and Ishmael have been sent away (21:8-20), so Isaac has been brought up as the only son and heir of Abraham in the protected and safe environment of Abraham's home. It is apparent that Abraham is now seen as a force to be reckoned with in the land of the Philistines. He is seen as a mighty prince (23:6), wealthy (24:35), a successful warrior (14:17), a prophet (20:7), and, significantly, a man under divine protection and blessing (21:22). Abraham had been obedient to the call of God and through that obedience God had been teaching him about himself. Abraham's relationship with God deepened (21:33) as he was now brought to the supreme test, learning the truth of Proverbs 3:11-12.

22:1 'Some time later' - the age of Isaac is uncertain, whether a young boy, youth or young man. Youth is more likely.

22:2 Isaac is the only son so far as concerns the promise. Abraham felt fatherly affection towards Ishmael (21:11), but it is clear that Isaac had a special place in Abraham's heart.

Moriah was the place where Solomon would build the Temple in Jerusalem (2 Chronicles 3:1). In New Testament times this was the vicinity of Calvary.

'Sacrifice him' - Abraham knew God as the eternal creator God, the one true God and he knew God's power in judgment (19:25). He also knew God to be trustworthy and merciful (18:32). It is unclear to what extent he knew other aspects of God's character, namely his morality and justice, which are inconsistent with anything arbitrary or unreasonable in his nature.

22:3 'Early' - see also 21:14. It infers a habit of facing a hard task resolutely.

22:4 'Third day' - consistent with the travel time from Beersheba to Jerusalem.

22:6 Loading of wood on to Isaac - see John 19:17 for the parallel with Jesus carrying his own cross.

22:8 'God himself will provide' - It is unclear whether Abraham still believed that God would intervene at the last minute. More probably this was the prophetic voice of Abraham. Hebrews 11:17-19 reveals that Abraham was expecting Isaac to be resurrected.

22:9 'Bound his son' - almost certainly Isaac must have submitted to his father's will. Here we see God's pattern for the chosen 'seed' to be a servant sacrificed.

22:10-12 Abraham demonstrated that he was prepared to sacrifice his son. Then God stepped in to prevent any harm coming to Isaac.

22:15-18 Abraham's faith was rewarded. But, note that the promised blessing was a confirmation of God's earlier covenant promise to Abraham. His faith was thus a means through which God worked to guarantee the gift he had already given. Therefore, Abraham's faith and obedience showed that there can be no blessing or benefit from God's saving grace without the believer's response. This was the pattern used by the New Testament writers (see Romans 4 and Hebrews 11). Behind and around this is the gracious call and mercy of God who provides the way for sins to be dealt with.

1. God tested Abraham by asking him to do a very hard thing. Discuss the sort of things that God might ask you to do to show that you put him first.

2. God provided a ram in place of Isaac. Compare this with Jesus' death on the cross on our behalf.

Who Came First? Run a quiz on the theme of 'who came first?'

E.G. Who was the first person to walk on the moon? (Neil Armstrong).

Who was the first person to run a mile in under 4 minutes? (Roger Bannister).

Who invented the first steam train? (George Stevenson).

You could also include more up-to-date firsts such as 'Who is first in the pop singles chart?', 'Who is currently first in the specified football league?'

You could also include questions specific to the group such as, 'Who arrived first today?', 'Who was born first out of everybody present?'

The quiz can be done as individuals or in teams. Offering prizes would introduce a more competitive element.

Point out that the exercise introduced the idea of being or coming first. Let's look at the Bible to see what happened when God asked Abraham to put him first.

Photocopy page 26 for each member of the group.

God tested Abraham, who, as a result, learnt an important lesson. Answer the following questions to discover what it was. The answers have been broken into groups of letters which will be found in the grid. As you answer each question cross off the relevant letters. The number in brackets refers to the number of letters in the answer. The first question has been done to start you off.

LY	THE	CK	BE	WO	NT
BOU	DO	~~MOR~~	LOR	AL	NK
BUR	ET	EY	THI	TH	DWI
LLP	EAR	ROV	OD	ND	SHE
BA	TAR	ER	REE	IDE	~~IAH~~

1. Where was Abraham told to take Isaac? (6)   MORIAH
2. What type of offering was Abraham to make? (5)
3. What time did Abraham get up? (5)
4. How many days did Abraham's journey take? (5)
5. What were the servants told to stay with? (6)
6. What did Isaac carry? (4)
7. What did Abraham build? (5)
8. What did Abraham do to Isaac before placing him on the altar? (5)
9. Where was the ram caught by its horns? (7)
10. Where did Abraham go afterwards? (9)

Now, reading from left to right and top to bottom, write the remaining groups of letters in order into the spaces below to discover what Abraham learnt.

_ _ _   _ _ _ _   _ _ _ _   _ _ _ _ _ _ _

PREPARATION
Genesis 24:1-67

LESSON AIMS
To learn that God guides those who obey him.

Abraham's life has been marked by a deepening relationship with the God who first called him and made himself known to him. At the base of that relationship is the covenant God has made with him, promising that through his son, Isaac, God would make of Abraham a great nation. Isaac having now grown into manhood, the time has come to marry in order to secure the line of descent. But Abraham's family is alone amongst a people (the Canaanites), whose outlook and culture is completely alien to all thought of God. It is clear, therefore, to Abraham that a Canaanite wife is not God's will for Isaac. It is equally clear that Isaac should not return to the land of his relatives, leaving the land of promise to which Abraham has been called. Once again, Abraham has to trust that God will guide and provide. Through his past experiences Abraham has learnt that God is trustworthy and could be trusted in his present situation (v.7).

24:1 Abraham was 140 years old and unaware that he had many years ahead of him. He died aged 175 (25:7). Sarah had died three years previously, when Isaac was 37. Isaac was 40 when he married Rebekah (25:20).

24:2 The chief servant demonstrated all the characteristics of a good servant with his common sense (v.5), his piety (v.26,52), his devotion to his master (v.12,14,27) and his resolve to follow his master's instructions as speedily as possible (v.33,56).

'the thigh' - this marked an extremely solemn vow.

24:3 Although Abraham had been living peacefully with the Canaanites for some while, he had already been taught by God that they would be enemies of his descendants (22:17), and were doomed to destruction.

Note that this was the beginning of God's people being told not to marry those who are not God's people (see Deuteronomy 7:3-4, 1 Kings 11:4, Ezra 9:1, 1 Corinthians 7:39).

24:8 Appropriately, Abraham's last quoted words in the Bible are words of faith in the Lord's faithfulness to his promises.

24:10 Nahor was probably the city of Haran, the place where Nahor's family had settled (v.24. Cf. Genesis 29:4-6). For the site, see the map on page 10.

The camels and other gifts would help conclude the marriage arrangements and were also sufficient evidence of Abraham's wealth to provide an inducement to the prospective bride.

24:12 The servant, as a circumcised member of Abraham's household, was within the covenant relationship (see 17:9-14). The servant's prayer of faith is linked to a practical purpose - to identify the girl with a generous and good-hearted attitude. His prayer is geared to special circumstances and the method should not be seen as normative any more than that of the disciples in Acts 1:24-26.

24:15 God's answer surpasses the prayer, which was being answered even as the servant prayed. After a moment's hesitation (v.21), the servant realised Rebekah was God's perfect answer to his prayer. Not only was she beautiful but she was also the granddaughter of Abraham's brother. No wonder he felt humbled and fell down in worship (v.26-27).

24:33 Note his reaction here and in v.56. He had to complete Abraham's commission without any delay that might jeopardise its success. At v.33 he was probably also bubbling with excitement at seeing God at work in his mission.

24:50-51 Rebekah's family could see that Abraham had received divine protection and blessing.

27

The servant's description of what had happened on the journey reinforced in their minds the fact that there had been supernatural intervention. It was from the Lord.

They use the name Yahweh (v.50), which indicates at least a knowledge of covenant faithfulness/promise. They were probably syncretistic, as their descendants became in Canaan after the conquest. They worshipped Yahweh and other gods - hence Exodus 20:3!

Note. This whole passage is an illustration of Proverbs 3:6 'In all your ways acknowledge him, and he will direct your paths.'

1. Are there any lessons we can learn from these verses about God's guidance?

2. Abraham's servant prays very specifically (v.12-14). So does Gideon in Judges 6:36-40. Are these a pattern that we should follow when seeking to know God's will?

Blindfolded Obstacle Course. Create an obstacle course out of tables and chairs in the room that you normally use. (The course does not have to be very large.) Ask the group to divide into pairs and blindfold one member of each pair. The blindfolded person has to make their way through the obstacle course being guided verbally by their partner. Once they have finished the course they can swap roles.

You might want to introduce an element of competition by timing people through the course. It may be possible to introduce an element of risk by placing cups of water or plates of shaving foam around the course.

At the end of the exercise point out that some guides were more trustworthy than others. Let's look at the Bible to see how God guided Abraham's servant.

Photocopy page 29, one for each member of the group. The Bible verse is Genesis 24:48.

Abraham's servant was sent to Haran to get a wife for Isaac. When the letters in each column are correctly positioned in the boxes above them, you will see what the servant said to Laban.

One letter has been placed to help you on your way.

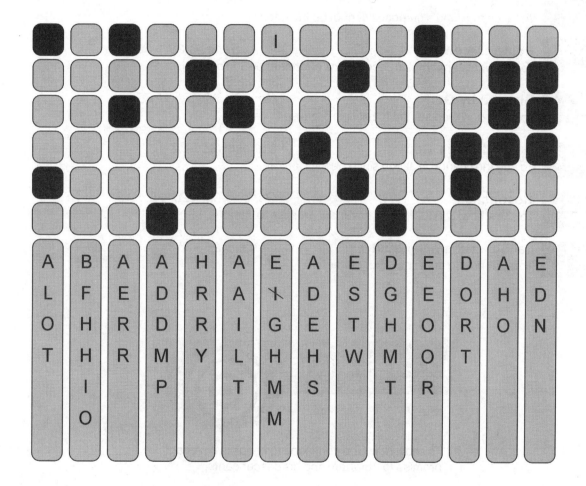

Which verse is this statement from?

OVERVIEW
Jacob

Week 8	**Deceiving**	*Genesis 25:19-34; 26:34 - 27:41*
	To teach that deceit and selfishness always lead to unhappiness and displease God.	

Week 9	**Dreaming**	*Genesis 27:41 - 28:22*
	To teach that God's purposes cannot be thwarted.	

Week 10	**Being Deceived**	*Genesis 29:1-30*
	To see what happened to Jacob in the aftermath of God's promise.	

Week 11	**Blessed by God**	*Genesis 30:25 - 31:55*
	To show how God started to fulfil his promise to Jacob.	

Week 12	**Depending on God**	*Genesis 32:1-32*
	To see the change in Jacob since he left Canaan.	

Week 13	**Reconciled**	*Genesis 33:1-20; 35:1-15*
	To show how God fulfilled his covenant promise to Jacob.	

Week 14	**Jacob - a character study**	*Genesis 25 - 35*
	To learn how to do a character study.	

SERIES AIMS

1. To show how God continued to keep his covenant promise to Abraham and his descendants.

2. To see the development of Jacob's relationship with God and the change this wrought in his character.

MEMORY WORK

Will not the Judge of all the earth do right?

Genesis 18:25

Jacob

When Isaac was 60 years old his wife had twin sons, Esau and Jacob (Genesis 25:24-26). Jacob lived during the 18th century BC and his name means 'he clutches'. Jacob grew up in a family where relationships were poor. Isaac preferred Esau, the extrovert hunter, because he enjoyed eating the animals that Esau caught, whereas Rebekah preferred Jacob, the quiet one who stayed at home (25:27-28).

The story starts with God telling Rebekah that the 2 children yet to be born would grow up to become 2 nations and that the older would serve the younger (25:23). The action then moves on to a time when the boys were grown up. Jacob was at home cooking soup when Esau returned from hunting feeling very hungry. He asked Jacob for soup. Jacob, seizing this opportunity, offered to give Esau the soup in exchange for the birthright (the right of the firstborn son to inherit more of the paternal estate than each of the other children). Esau agreed and the exchange was made. Neither brother demonstrated godly behaviour in this episode - Jacob showed no generosity or concern for others, and Esau showed how little he regarded his position as the firstborn son (25:34).

This episode is followed by the story of Isaac determining to give his blessing to Esau (27:1-4). Rebekah over-heard Isaac's plan and encouraged Jacob to deceive his father and obtain the blessing for himself (27:5-10). In spite of God's promise to her before the children were born (25:23), Rebekah was not prepared to trust God to work it out. The plan succeeded and Esau was furious. He determined to kill Jacob once Isaac was dead (27:41).

Rebekah sent Jacob away to Haran in Mesopotamia to her own family to get a wife. On his way he spent the night at Bethel where God appeared to him in a dream and repeated the promise he made to Abraham (12:3; 13:14-15; 22:18). God also promised Jacob to be with him, to protect him wherever he went, and to bring him back to Canaan (28:13-15). Jacob's response at this stage was - if you will keep your promise, then you will be my God (28:20-22).

Jacob then journeyed on to Haran and met up with Rebekah's family. He fell in love with Rachel, Laban's younger daughter, and agreed to work for 7 years for the right to marry her. However, when the time came for the wedding, Laban tricked Jacob into marrying her elder sister, Leah. Jacob took Rachel as his second wife and worked a further 7 years for Laban, during which time God blessed Jacob with children and wealth.

Jacob continued to work for Laban. Some years later God appeared to Jacob again and told him to return to Canaan (31:3). Jacob was still the deceiver and planned to leave for Canaan when his father-in-law was away from home (31:17-21). On his way back to Israel 'he struggled with God' (32:22-30). Following this Jacob changed and his trust in God became evident (33:11,20; 35:1-15).

In this series we see how the same God, who promised Abraham that he would be the father of many nations and through him all nations would be blessed (12:1-3), promised Jacob that he would be with him and would protect him wherever he went (28:13-15). This God is not only concerned with the destinies of nations but also with the care of the individual. We will also see how Jacob's relationship with God developed and learn that, in his case as in ours, it was due to God's sovereign grace alone.

PREPARATION

Genesis
25:19-34;
26:34 - 27:41

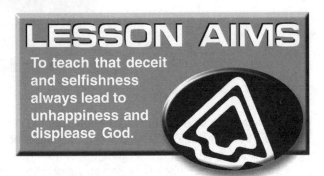

LESSON AIMS

To teach that deceit and selfishness always lead to unhappiness and displease God.

25:23 Note God's promise to Rebekah that the younger twin would be the heir.

25:25 Esau is a name pun on the Hebrew word for hairy. Edom (v.30) means red.

25:26 Jacob sounds like the Hebrew word for heel. The twins were born 20 years after Isaac and Rebekah were married (see v.20).

25:28 Note the favouritism - Isaac preferred Esau and Rebekah preferred Jacob. The group needs to be reminded that favouritism is wrong.

25:31 The birthright belonged to the firstborn son and included a larger inheritance, special paternal blessing, family leadership and an honoured place at mealtimes. In later times the firstborn son received a double share of the inheritance (Deuteronomy 21:15-17).

25:31-35 Neither twin comes out of this episode with honour. Jacob demonstrated a mean spirit and Esau showed his lack of concern for future privileges.

26:34 Esau married outside the covenant.

27:1-10 Both Isaac's and Rebekah's actions stem from the early favouritism shown in 25:28. Although God had promised Rebekah that Jacob would be the heir, she did not trust God to do what he had promised. We do not know whether or not Isaac was aware of this promise (25:23).

27:11-12 Jacob's qualms about the proposed course of action were pragmatic, not moral.

27:20 Jacob is even prepared to use God's name to help in the deceit.

27:33 The paternal blessing was irrevocable.

27:36 Supplanted comes from the Hebrew 'to take by the heel' (25:26).

QUESTIONS

1. When Rebekah could not have children Isaac prayed about it. How long did it take God to answer (v.26)? What sort of things do we pray about? How quickly do we give up and why?

2. What was wrong with the behaviour of Esau and Jacob in 25:29-32? What does this tell us about the home situation and Esau's view of his family and of God?

3. God's Law tells us to obey our parents (Exodus 20:12, Ephesians 6:1). Does this excuse Jacob from blame for deceiving his father?

Cheat Play the card game, 'Cheat' in a large group. Use 1 pack for up to 6 players, 2 packs for 7-12 players and 3 packs for over 12 players. Shuffle the packs and deal out all the cards. All players should have the same number of cards, so discard any left over.

The aim of the game is to be the first person to discard all their cards. The dealer starts by placing a card face down in the centre and announcing it's rank, e.g. 'a 9'. Play moves clockwise round the table. The next player places a card face down on top of the previous card, announcing the rank immediately above the previous one, e.g. 'a 10'. Continue to King, Ace, 2, etc.

Any player may cheat by playing a different card from the one they announce. After a card has been played and announced, any player(s) may challenge by calling out 'Cheat'. A referee may be needed to say who challenged first! The top card is then turned over. If the player did cheat he has to take the whole pile of cards from the centre of the table. If he did not cheat the challenger takes the cards.

Alternatively, find a story in the local or national press of deceiving, e.g. a conman, disguised as a Gas Meter reader, who gets let into an elderly person's home and steals their pension book or savings. Discuss the story, the deceit, how the victim felt, how the conman should be punished.

Let's look at the Bible to see what happened when someone cheated members of his family.

This passage is a good one for acting out. The group is split in half and asked to prepare a play from the passage to act to each other. The play can be either the Bible story or a modern adaptation. Each group is responsible for organising themselves. They should appoint a director, who can then decide with his/her group on the script, apportion parts, etc.

Suggested props: sunglasses for Isaac, fleecy for putting over Jacob's arms.

PREPARATION

Genesis 27:41 - 28:22

LESSON AIMS

To teach that God's purposes cannot be thwarted.

27:45   Rebekah died before Jacob returned from Haran (see 49:29-32).

27:46   Note the way Rebekah approached both Jacob and Isaac - asking both to consider her happiness, but using different arguments for each.

28:6-9   Some indication of Esau's spiritual state can be gained from his reaction to learning what Isaac said about Canaanite women. He takes another wife from the family of Ishmael, who is also outside God's covenant with Abraham.

28:13-15   God confirms the covenant blessing made by Isaac - a repeat of the promise made to Abraham (12:2-3; 13:15-17; 17:4-8; 22:15-18).

28:19   Bethel = house of God.

28:20-22   Jacob ratifies the covenant with a vow of allegiance (v.22) - if God will do as he has promised Jacob will be his servant.

The stairway extended from earth to heaven. This is different from the stairways on the ziggurats (artificial temple mounds), which were supposed to lead from the gods' dwelling place at the top to the earth below. (The tower of Babel was a ziggurat).

2. Compare God's promise to Jacob (28:13-15) with his promise to Abraham (12:1-3; 13:14-15; 22:18). What does this teach us about God?

3. What does 28:20-22 tell us about Jacob's relationship with God?

FOCUS ACTIVITY

Dreamers   Ask the young people if any of them dream? Can they remember their dreams? Point out that, in Bible times, sometimes dreams had meanings. Today we will look at a very special dream.

Start by filling in Jacob's family tree as a class activity (see pages 35 and 36). Either photocopy it or reproduce it on a flip chart. Use the following Bible verses to help fill in the gaps: Genesis 11:27-29; 16:1-2,15; 24:15,24; 29:16. Use the completed family tree as a visual aid and explanation for this story and others in the series.

ACTIVITY

Photocopy page 37, one for each member of the group. The Bible verse is Genesis 18:25.

QUESTIONS

1. What was the significance of Jacob's dream as he was on his way to Haran (28:10-15)?

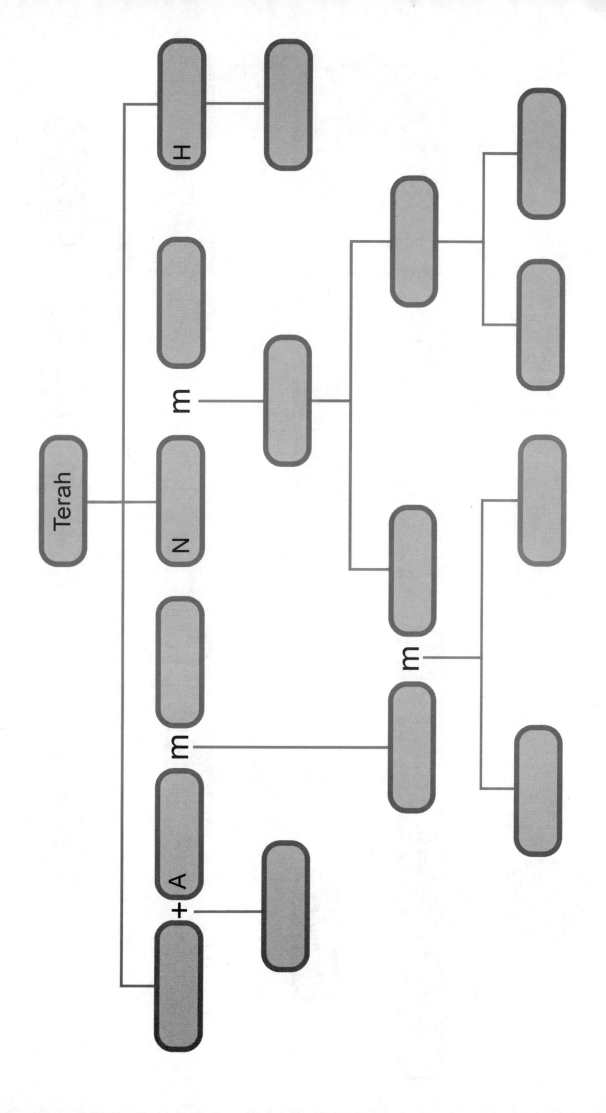

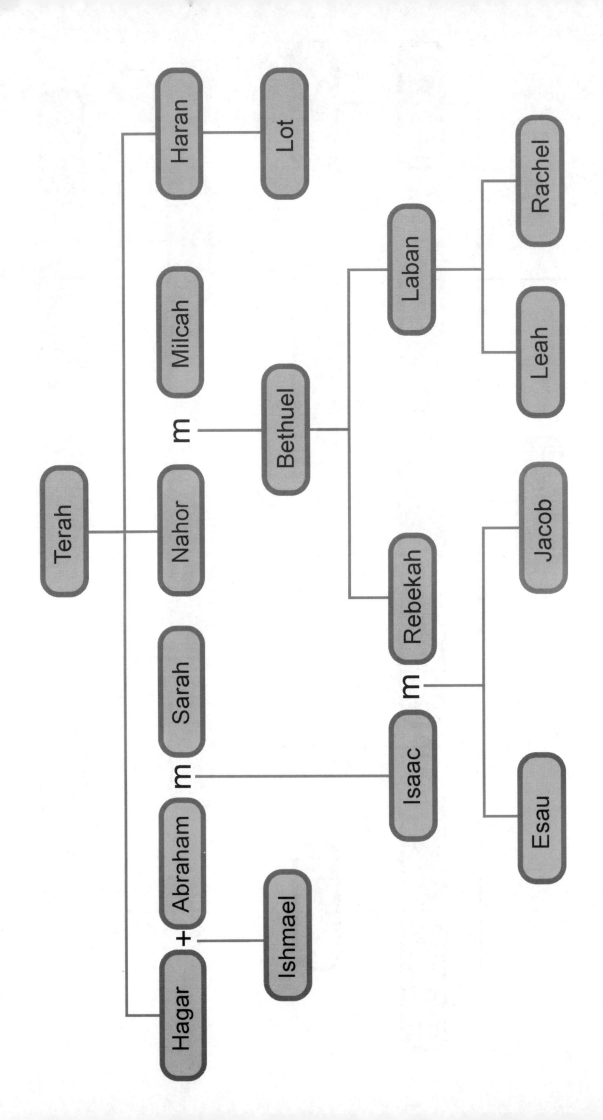

Fit the jigsaw pieces into the frame provided to discover what Jacob needed to know about God. The words run straight after each other with no breaks in between. The shaded squares should help to get you started.

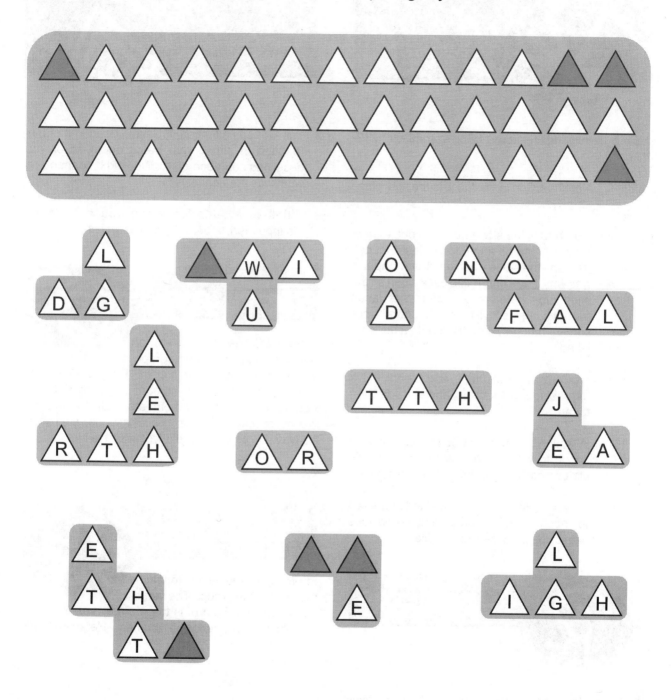

Where does this verse come from?

PREPARATION
Genesis 29:1-30

LESSON AIMS
To see what happened to Jacob in the aftermath of God's promise.

Start by reminding the group of God's promise (28:13-15).

29:2 Note how God leads Jacob to the right place (cf. v.4).

29:10 Jacob rolls the stone back (in defiance of local custom) as a feat to impress Rachel. Perhaps the stone was very heavy and this was why it was only rolled back when all the shepherds were present. Note that Jacob did not have the lavish gifts that Abraham's servant brought when he sought a bride for Isaac.

29:14 'you are my own flesh and blood' - this expression is found in ancient adoption forms.

29:15 Although Laban sounds generous, by asking Jacob to work for pay he is reducing his status from family member to hired servant.

29:30 14 years have passed since God appeared to Jacob at Bethel and there is no obvious sign of the promise being fulfilled.

2. Think of any situation you have been in that has resulted in either your being deceived or you deceiving someone else. Why did it happen and what was the end result?

3. Think of a situation when you have been disappointed. How did you deal with it?

FOCUS ACTIVITY

Family Likeness. Ask each leader to bring in a photograph of a parent or themselves as a child. Display the photos and give the group a set amount of time to match up leaders with their family members. Talk about family likenesses and lead into the Bible passage being about the way one of Jacob's relatives was like him.

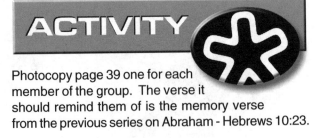

ACTIVITY

Photocopy page 39 one for each member of the group. The verse it should remind them of is the memory verse from the previous series on Abraham - Hebrews 10:23.

QUESTIONS

1. Laban deceived Jacob in the matter of his wife. Was this rough justice? (Remember how Jacob deceived Isaac.)

Things were not going right for Jacob. Could God be trusted to keep his promise of Genesis 28:13-15?

With the help of the clues on the right, add one letter to each of the words on the left to make a new word. Place the new letter in the box provided. Then write the letters in the boxes into the space below to give the answer.

Word		Clue
IT	☐	Jesus makes us this for heaven
PRY	☐	how we communicate with God
PLAN	☐	make it clear
SAND	☐	What you do when you get up
OUR	☐	60 minutes
ARM	☐	a place where you may find sheep
FOR	☐	a number
PUMP	☐	not really fat

The Lord is _ _ _ _ _ _ _ _ to all his promises. Psalm 145:13

Which other verse in the Bible does this remind you of ?

Hebrews 10:23

PREPARATION

Genesis
30:25 - 31:55

LESSON AIMS

To show how God started to fulfil his promise to Jacob.

29:31 to 30:24 This section needs to be summarised - the group needs to know that Jacob had 4 'wives' ('as the custom was in those days') and had 12 children - 11 sons and 1 daughter. It also needs pointing out that the home situation was very unhappy as a result of the 2 sisters competing for the attention of their husband.

30:25 Jacob's 14 years of service were over.

30:34-36 Laban does all in his power to prevent Jacob taking what had been agreed in v.31-33.

30:37-43 God overrules and blesses Jacob as he has promised (28:15).

31:1 Laban's sons were his heirs and saw their inheritance being whittled away.

31:3 God tells Jacob it is time to return to Canaan. (Cf. God's promise to bring Jacob back to Canaan in 28:15).

31:4 Jacob is still a schemer. Rather than speak to his wives in their tents, where they may have been overheard, he calls them out to the open field.

31:5-13 Jacob sees God's hand in all that has happened.

31:19 Rachel shows that she is no different from her father or husband.

31:20 Even though God has told Jacob to leave, Jacob does not go openly.

31:24 God continues to look after Jacob (see also v.29).

31:38 It was 20 years since Jacob left Canaan. He had worked a further 6 years for Laban since the conversation in 30:25-34.

31:44 Jacob and Laban make a covenant. This would have been a parity covenant (see notes on covenants in week 3).

31:47 Both names mean 'witness heap'.

31:49 Mizpah means 'watchtower'.

QUESTIONS

1. In 2 Timothy 3:16 we read why **all** Scripture is useful. With that verse in mind why has God given us the passage in Genesis 31?

2. Did Jacob's actions in this week's passage demonstrate his trust in God? How should we behave in difficult situations?

FOCUS ACTIVITY

All Change Divide the group into pairs. Give each pair two drinking straws and a sweet with a hole in the middle. The pairs face each other in a long line. Everyone puts the straw into their mouth and one of the pair places the sweet over the straw. On the command, 'All change!' the pairs have to transfer the sweet from one straw to the other without touching the straw or sweet with their hands. Change pairings and repeat.

Recap on Jacob's character. Remind the group how difficult some of them found it to change the sweet from one straw to the other. It is even more difficult to change as a person. Let's look at the Bible to see whether Jacob has changed.

ACTIVITY

Look up the notes on covenants in week 3. Apply the covenant form to the covenant between Jacob and Laban (31:44-54).

PREPARATION

Genesis 32:1-32

LESSON AIMS

To see the change in Jacob since he left Canaan.

32:1   Cf. 28:12-15.

32:2   Mahanaim means '2 camps'. The 2 camps could refer to the angels and Jacob's company.

32:7-12   Jacob takes sensible precautions as well as trusting God.

32:9-12   Jacob's prayer demonstrates the change that has taken place in him since leaving home - he now depends on God for his salvation.

32:13-21   The fact of Jacob's dependence on God does not prevent him using wisdom in his dealings with Esau.

32:22-24   Jacob sends his family across the Jabbok into Canaan but he stays behind.

         The man who wrestled with Jacob was God (see vv.28, 30).

32:25   The hip/thigh was considered to be the seat of reproductive powers - so the smiting was symbolic of the smiting of one of Jacob's descendants (Isaiah 53:4). Blessing was achieved through suffering.

32:31   Peniel = the face of God.

QUESTIONS

1. Think back to Jacob's behaviour at the beginning of this series. How is he different in this chapter?

2. Jacob's name was changed to Israel (v.28). In what ways had he struggled with God and with men and overcome?

FOCUS ACTIVITY

My, how you've changed! Ask everyone to write down a funny or embarassing thing that happened to them as a child and then to say how they have changed since then. They do not put their names on the paper to avoid any embarrassment. Put all the papers in the middle, shuffle them and hand them out. Go round the group reading them out. Let's look at the Bible to see how Jacob has changed.

ACTIVITY

Charades (Give us a clue)

Prior to the lesson choose suitable verses or words from the Bible passage for acting out. Split the group into 2 teams. Allocate each team a number of words or verses. The teams take it in turn to act out the words or verse to the other side. Points are scored by the teams for correct answers.

Use the following actions to indicate what is being acted:

Word - bring hand away from mouth once.

Verse - bring the hand away from mouth then starting with the hands together in front of the mouth, part the hands to demonstrate length i.e. more than one word.

This activity can also be done using drawings rather than actions.

WEEK 13

Reconciled

PREPARATION

Genesis
33:1-20; 35:1-15

LESSON AIMS

To show how God
fulfilled his covenant
promise to Jacob.

33:3   Bowing 7 times was homage to a king.

33:11   By accepting the gift Esau would be demonstrating that he acquiesced in Jacob's inheritance.

33:14   Note that Jacob told Esau he would join him at Seir but Jacob went to Succoth (v.17).

33:17   Succoth = shelters.

33:18   There was a period of some years between v.17 and v.18.

33:20   El Elohe Israel means 'God, the God of Israel'.

35:1   This follows on from the incident with Dinah (34:1-31). God protects Jacob and his family by moving him to another site.

35:2-3   Jacob and his family prepare for Jacob's fulfilment of his vow in 28:20-22. God was to be worshipped exclusively. Note the need for ritual purification. (Cf. Exodus 19:10.)

35:8   Allon Bacuth means 'oak of weeping'.

35:10-13   God renews his covenant with Jacob.

FOCUS ACTIVITY

Find Your Partner   Prior to the lesson write onto adhesive labels the names of famous couples, one name per label, e.g. Queen Elizabeth II and Prince Philip. Use fictional as well as real characters. Stick a label onto the back of each group member. The aim of the game is for each person to be 'reconciled' with their partner. They do this by asking each other questions, which can only be answered with 'yes' or 'no'. Allow about ten minutes for the exercise then see who has been reconciled and who has not. Let's see what the Bible has to say about the way Jacob was reconciled with his brother.

QUESTIONS

1. Read 28:13-15. How has God fulfilled his promise to Jacob?

2. At the renewal of the covenant in 35:10-13 does God make the same promises? How do these compare with the promises made to Abraham (12:1-3; 13:14-15; 22:15-18).

VISUAL AID

A map is useful to show Jacob's journey from Haran to Canaan (see page 10).

ACTIVITY

Photocopy page 44 for each member of the group.

Quick Quiz!

Answer the questions and enter your answers in the grid.

1. Jacob had 13 of them.

2. The type of tree where Jacob buried the idols.

3. The opposite of defeat.

4. Jacob's brother.

5. What will come from Jacob? (35:11).

6. How Jacob felt before meeting his brother (32:11).

7. The second word of your memory verse.

8. Jacob's great grandfather.

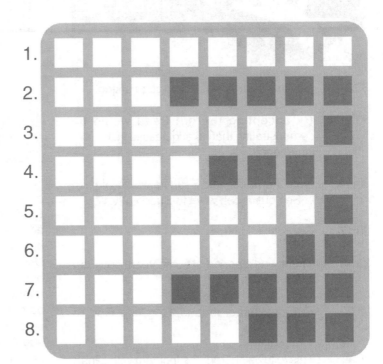

The letters in the first columm spell _ _ _ _ _ _ _ _ .

WEEK 14
Jacob - a character study

PREPARATION

Genesis 25 - 35

LESSON AIMS

To learn how to do a character study.

As they get older the group will need to be taught a variety of Bible study skills to equip them to study the Bible for themselves. This week demonstrates how to study a character. There is a lot of material to cover so it may be wise to split the group into smaller units, giving each unit one section to look at. The information gained can be pooled at the end in table form on a board/flip chart.

The information required

1. Family details, e.g. names of parents, brothers and sisters, etc.

   Genesis 25:20-21,24-26,28; 27:41; 29:23,28; Genesis 29:31 - 30:28 for details of wives and children.

2. Place and type of dwelling.

   Genesis 25:27; 28:2; 31:18; 33:17-20; 35:1

3. Occupation and abilities/talents.

   Genesis 25:29; 30:29-31

4. Details of character, e.g. quiet and home loving.

   Genesis 25:27-28; 27:5-26; 29:18; 30:25-30,33; 31:25-31

5. Major events, e.g. sent to Haran because his brother threatened to kill him.

   Genesis 25:23; 27:1-29; 28:10-22; 31:19-21,44-54; 32:22-32; 33:1-20; 35:9-15

6. Strong points, e.g. honest (31:38-39).

   Genesis 28:5,16-22; 29:16-18; 31:5,38-42; 32:7-12; 35:1-4

7. Weak points, e.g. deceiver (27:35; 31:20).

   Genesis 25:27-34; 27:5-26,35; 31:20,25-31

8. What can we learn from this to help us walk more closely with God?

FOCUS ACTIVITY

Who do you know? Give the group the name of a famous person (real or fictional), whom they should know something about. Ask them what they know, each person giving one piece of information. Then ask the group members to take it in turns to state what they know about the person on their left. Which was the easier activity and why? Lead in to the character study.

OVERVIEW
The Messiah

Week 15   **The Messiah Foretold**   *Isaiah 9:1-7; 11:1-10; 53:1-9*
To discover more about the Messiah's birth, kingdom, and suffering.

Week 16   **The Incarnation**   *John 1:1-18*
To understand more about the truth that Jesus became man.

SERIES AIMS

1. To see the direct link between the Old and the New Testaments and how the prophecy was fulfilled in Jesus.

2. To understand more of the incredible fact that God became man in Jesus Christ.

MEMORY WORK

In the beginning was the Word, and the Word was with God, and the Word was God. He was with God in the beginning.

John 1:1-2

The Messiah

Before Jesus was born, about 700 BC, the prophet Isaiah wrote about a Messiah, or anointed one, who would bring light into a dark world (9:2), who would come from the Davidic line (11:1), and who would be king (9:6-7). His rule would be characterised by righteousness, justice and peace (11:3-5), but the king would die for the sake of his people (53:4-9). The Messiah would be called 'Immanuel - God with us' (7:14).

In the prologue to John's Gospel, we see part of those prophecies fulfilled. The theme of light is developed and will be studied properly in the following series on the 7 sayings of Jesus in John's gospel. Jesus in the fullest sense became man, God with us, but suffered rejection by his own people.

PREPARATION

Isaiah
9:1-7; 11:1-10;
53:1-9

LESSON AIMS

To discover more about the Messiah's birth, kingdom and suffering.

Isaiah is the first of the prophetic books in the Old Testament and contains God's message to the southern kingdom of Judah. Isaiah was writing around the 8th century BC, during the reigns of Jotham, Ahaz and Hezekiah (Isaiah 1:1). His commission as a prophet came about 740 BC - 'in the year that King Uzziah died' (Isaiah 6:1-8). The exile was still in the future, although the northern kingdom of Israel fell to the Assyrians in 722 BC. At the time of writing Israel had been taken into exile and the Assyrians had overrun parts of Judah (Isaiah 1:7-9), and the general situation was one of religious, social and moral decay (Isaiah 1:2-17,21-23; 3:8-17; 5:8-23). In this time of darkness a Messiah is promised, who will be the son of David (Isaiah 11:1), whose kingdom would have no end (Isaiah 9:7) and who would be a light not only to the Jews but also to the Gentiles (Isaiah 9:1-2, Luke 2:29-32).

Perhaps, because these passages are so often read, their familiarity makes them harder to study, but they contain so many truths and promises that they bear careful attention.

Messiah's Birth - Isaiah 9:1-7

9:1   Zebulun and Naphtali were part of the northern kingdom of Israel and had already fallen to Assyria.

Galilee contained Nazareth, where Jesus grew up, and Cana, the site of the first miracle.

The way of the sea was the main road connecting Syria with Egypt. It passed through Galilee.

9:2   The land was in spiritual darkness (8:19-22) as well as under the threat of political invasion. The light points forward to Jesus, the light of the world (John 8:12).

9:3   Rejoicing and joy are brought by this Messiah. The verse talks about a time of peace and prosperity that were a complete contrast with their present situation.

9:4   Deliverance will come too, as Gideon delivered the people from the Midianites (Judges 6-7).

9:6   A child is named 700 years before his birth. 'Wonderful' is used regularly in Scripture to denote the supernatural, so this implies the divinity of the coming deliverer (see Isaiah 28:29).

9:6   'Counsellor' - the Messiah as king will carry out a programme of royal action planned long ago.

'Mighty God' - see Isaiah 10:20-21.

'Everlasting father' - his fatherly love and protection will last forever.

'Prince of Peace' - his rule will bring wholeness to both individuals and society (John 11:27).

Messiah's kingdom - Isaiah 11:1-10

11:1   Even though the kingdom of Judah had been cut down, from Jesse's family (David's father) a shoot will grow.

11:2   cf. John 1:33-34. The Spirit will come upon the Messiah. The Spirit and the Messiah are two persons of the Holy Trinity.

11:4-5 Righteousness and justice will characterise his reign, unlike the leaders of the time who lacked integrity.

11:6-9 Peace and safety will be there; no fear of harm or attack. This section speaks of the time when Jesus will come again in judgment.

11:10   'Root of Jesse' cf. v.1 and Revelation 5:5.

Messiah's Suffering - Isaiah 53:1-9

53:1   'Our message' - the good news of salvation given by the prophets.

53:2   David was fine-looking (1 Samuel 16:18), but Christ had none of this appeal.

53:3   Despised, rejected, a man of sorrows, familiar with suffering - all demonstrated fully on the cross and in the events leading up to Jesus' death.

53:4-5   Our infirmities, our sorrows, our transgressions, our iniquities were what he took on the cross.

53:6   'Laid on him the iniquity of us all' - just as the priest in Leviticus 16:21 laid his hands on the scapegoat to demonstrate the taking away of the people's sins, so Jesus took our sins away.

53:7   Matthew 27:12-14, Luke 23:8-9. Jesus remained silent before the chief priests and Pilate and before Herod.

Photocopy page 50 for each person.

1. When Jesus came to Palestine 700 years after those prophecies why did so many Jews not recognise him?

2. What type of ruler would they have preferred?

3. When Jesus comes again, how will it differ from his first coming? Philippians 2:6-11.

Photofit   Describe two men for the group to draw. Compare all the drawings to see how people have interpreted things differently, e.g. the different ways a moustache has been drawn. Link into looking at Isaiah's prophecies regarding the promised Messiah and how specific they were.

Look up the following references to discover titles used to depict Jesus and enter your answers in the grid. If you get it right the letters in the first column will spell a further title.

1) Isaiah 53:3   2) Isaiah 9:6   3) Daniel 7:13   4) Isaiah 62:11

5) Isaiah 7:14   6) Psalm 2:2   7) Mark 1:24

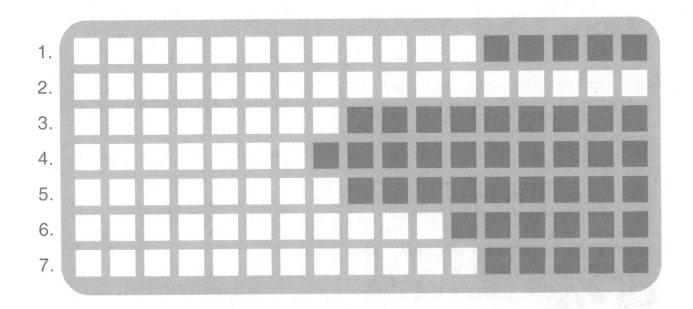

The letters in the first columm spell   _ _ _ _ _ _ _ .

What is the Greek form of this word?

PREPARATION

John 1:1-18

LESSON AIMS

To understand more of the truth that Jesus became man.

'Incarnation' is not a word frequently used, and it is one which the young people may need to think about. God took human form and became man for us. The Prologue, i.e. these first 18 verses, will introduce themes that will be studied in the following series on the 7 sayings of Jesus in John's gospel. Jesus as the Light, the Life and the Truth are all favourite topics of John.

1:1　　The Word was Jesus; he was there before the creation, cf. Genesis 1:1. These first 18 verses begin and end with the affirmation of his deity - 'the Word was God' (v.1), 'God the One and Only, who is at the Father's side' (v.18).

1:3　　He was active in creation.

1:4　　Light and Life are inseparable (cf. John 8:12).

1:6-7　　This is John the Baptist who was the witness to Jesus. His testimony was to Jesus, the Son of God (cf. 1:34).

1:9-10　　True light coming into the world. The world here could mean a number of things; the created universe, the people, people opposed to God, or systems opposed to God. The emphasis is given by repetition and moves from one to another without explanation.

1:11　　His own people, the Jews, rejected him.

1:12　　The right of membership of God's family is not earned, it is given (cf. Ephesians 2:8-9). It can never be achieved by human effort or wisdom. 'Received' and 'believed' make clear man's response to the gift.

1:14　　Jesus became flesh. The word existed before he became man. 'Dwelling' and 'glory' were terms that would point the Jewish reader to God's dwelling in the tabernacle where his glory was shown (Exodus 40:34-35).

Grace - the undeserved favour / mercy of God.

Truth - Jesus is the truth (14:6).

1:15　　Even though John the Baptist had died long before this gospel was written his teaching still rang true. He affirms the deity and supremacy of Christ.

QUESTIONS

1. Which carols, old and new, teach us something about the Incarnation?

2. Why did John call Jesus 'the Word'?

What's the connection? Divide the group into two teams. The teams take it in turns for one of their members to mime a word for their team to guess. A successful guess gains the team a point. If the team is unable to guess the word the opposing team is allowed a guess. Use words that have something to do with the theme of the Bible passage, e.g. word, candle, torch, witness, world, children, law.

Link into the Bible study by seeing what these words have to do with today's passage.

Photocopy page 53 for each person.

In the following word square are hidden 4 names, 1 time, 10 nouns and 3 verbs, all taken from today's Bible passage. The words run horizontally, vertically and diagonally and each word is allowed to change direction only once. At the end of each word an arrow indicates where the next word starts. You can begin at any arrow in the square. All the letters are used and no letter is used more than once.

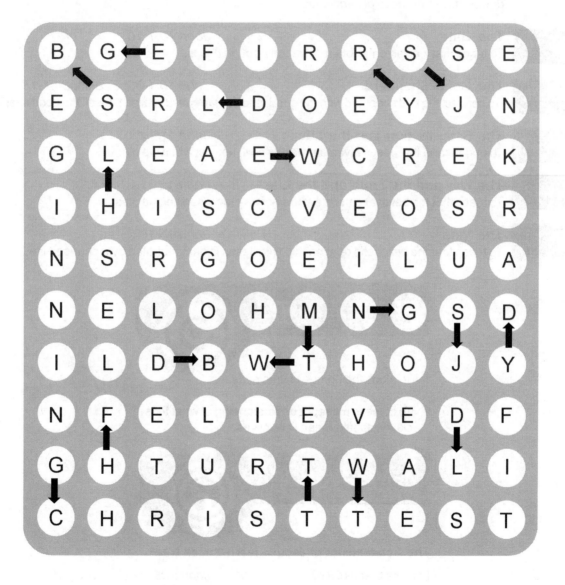

OVERVIEW
Jesus said: 'I am ...'

Week 17	**The Bread of Life**	*John 6:25-60*

To understand that Jesus promises eternal life to all who believe in him.

Week 18	**The Light of the World**	*John 8:12; 9:1-41; Ephesians 2:1-5; 5:8-14a*

To teach that Jesus exposes the darkness of sin, both in the world and in the individual, and thus demonstrates my need of forgiveness.

Week 19	**The Gate**	*John 10:1-10*

To teach that we can only obtain salvation through Jesus.

Week 20	**The Good Shepherd**	*John 10:1-30; Ezekiel 34:1-16*

To contrast the bad shepherd with the good, and see why Jesus called himself the good shepherd.

Week 21	**The Resurrection and the Life**	*John 11:1-44*

To understand that Jesus gives eternal life now, not just when we die.

Week 22	**The Way and the Truth and the Life**	*John 13:31 - 14:14*

To teach that the believer can be assured of heaven when he/she dies.

Week 23	**The Vine**	*John 15:1-17*

To teach that the believer's relationship with Jesus is demonstrated by a changed life.

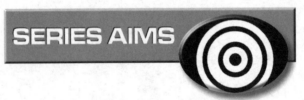

SERIES AIMS

1. To study the unique claims of Jesus.

2. To come to a deeper understanding of what those claims should mean in our lives.

MEMORY WORK

The 7 statements of Jesus - learn 1 each week.

I am the bread of life.	*John 6:35*
I am the light of the world.	*John 8:12*
I am the gate;	*John 10:9*
I am the good shepherd.	*John 10:11*
I am the resurrection and the life.	*John 11:25*
I am the way and the truth and the life.	*John 14:6*
I am the vine;	*John 15:5*

Jesus said: 'I am ...'

In his Gospel John has recorded 7 statements Jesus made about himself. In preparing the lessons for this series on the 7 'I am s' it is important to keep in mind the knowledge of the group. Some will come with a deeper level of understanding and this will have a bearing on the lesson preparation. John's Gospel is a very important theological treatise. Its language is simple, with very few long words, and with straightforward sentence construction. However, this can be deceptive, because the meaning is profound and sometimes provocative. John's aim in writing was evangelistic (20:31) '... that you may believe that Jesus is the Christ, the Son of God and that by believing you may have life in his name.'

The 7 'I am s' are a presentation of what Jesus came to be and to do. They are 'egocentric' in their teaching and point to the person of Jesus, e.g. he is not **giving** them bread, he **is** the bread; he **is** the light of the world. They are statements about a person, and sometimes begin with everyday pictures that the hearers can readily understand. Each passage contains an enormous amount of teaching and repays careful study. The unique claims of Jesus are shown in these passages and will come into conflict with what the young people are hearing all around them. It is considered arrogant today to be exclusive, but this is exactly what Jesus is teaching. Truth alone will save, not a belief system which has man's approval, and this will be hard for some young people (and adults) to accept.

PREPARATION

John 6:25-60

LESSON AIMS

To understand that Jesus promises eternal life to all who believe in him.

This passage follows on the miracle of the feeding of the five thousand. The crowds want more - they are preoccupied with signs and miracles.

6:26 The crowd are still looking for 'free handouts'.

6:27 'The seal of approval' - the seal was used to authenticate a document. The person who held the seal exercised the authority of the owner of the seal. **NB** The Father has given his authority to Jesus as Son of Man.

6:28 In that culture there would have been a direct link between work and food - they had to work to eat. Here the point is missed, that eternal life is a gift not an achievement.

6:29 The work God requires is belief in Jesus.

6:30-32 They still want a sign, in spite of the feeding of the 5,000! They seem to equate Jesus with Moses as a prophet (cf. v.14) and ask him to give them a similar sign to Moses giving the manna.

6:33 The true bread of God is not manna but a person.

6:34 A materialistic demand - 'Give us this bread.' They miss the point.

6:35 Here is the first of the 7 'I am s'. Solemn words with a reminder of the 'I am who I am' of Exodus 3:14.

6:36-40 A development of who the 'Bread of Life' really is, Jesus himself - eternal life which gives full, lasting satisfaction and the security which even death cannot shake. God's action, not man's, is the pre-requisite for salvation (v.37); it is his work of drawing man to himself. See John 17:3 for an explanation of eternal life.

6:40 Cf. Numbers 21:8-9 and John 3:14-15.

6:41-42 After these startling revelations, the Jews start debating the claims of Jesus by referring to his human origins.

6:43-45 The doctrine of election will be studied in detail in Book 3.

6:49-50 Their forefathers died even though they ate the bread of heaven, but Jesus gives eternal, lasting life that doesn't die.

6:51-57 A pointing towards the Last Supper and Crucifixion.

6:52 The Jews take it literally - 'How can we eat this flesh?'

6:60 They couldn't accept that hard teaching of Jesus.

QUESTIONS

1. What is eternal life?

2. How do we eat Jesus' flesh and drink his blood (v.53)?

Food for Thought. Ask the group to spend a couple of minutes thinking about the following question: '*If you could only eat your favourite food for the rest of your life, what would it be?*' Then play a game along the lines of 'My Aunt Went to Market'. The first person begins with the phrase, 'If I could eat my favourite food every day for the rest of my life it would be ...' and adds their food item. Continue round the group with each person repeating what the previous person has said and adding their own food item onto the end of the list. The winner is the person who can remember everyone's favourite food item. Point out that Jesus said that he is the Bread of Life. Let's look at the Bible to see what that means.

Divide the group into units of 4/5 and ask them to provide a television news report on 'Recent happenings in Jerusalem'. They will need a news reader, an on-the-spot reporter and 2/3 witnesses. Give the groups time to prepare and then get each one to present their report to the rest of the class.

PREPARATION

John 8:12; 9:1-41,
Ephesians 2:1-5;
5:8-14a

LESSON AIMS

To teach that Jesus exposes the darkness of sin in the world and individual, thus demonstrating my need of forgiveness.

These passages show the total darkness of sin and the fact that men prefer darkness to light, because it shows up their evil deeds (John 3:19). John 9:1-41 should be a quick revision of the story, with the emphasis being on the last few verses (35-41), which show that spiritual rather than the physical blindness is the main theme of the passage.

John

9:2   This is a reference to the rabbinical teaching that individuals were punished by illness or death for sin they committed.

9:3   Of course the man and his parents were sinners, but Jesus is contradicting the rabbis' teaching of the previous verse.

9:4   'The night is coming' - it was important to continue the work whilst Jesus was still with them as the light of the world (John 9:5; 8:12). In John's gospel night/darkness often refers to the spiritual state. Some Christians think that the state of darkness refers to the time between the cross and Pentecost - Jesus was taken from them and they were not yet empowered by the Holy Spirit.

9:5   'The light of the world' - the OT bore witness to the Messiah being a light for the people walking in darkness (Isaiah 9:2-7; 42:1-7). All unbelievers are in a state of spiritual blindness/darkness from which only God can release them (2 Corinthians 4:4-6, 1 Peter 2:9).

9:16   The absurdity of the Pharisees' laws; God couldn't possibly work on the Sabbath!

9:35 - 41   The emphasis here is on spiritual blindness even in those who were the religious leaders.

9:39   Jesus speaks to the man who has been healed, but it must have been in a public place because he was overheard by some Pharisees (9:40). The coming of Jesus was to save (John 3:17) but the presentation of the gospel, whilst saving some, causes offence to others. The blind are those who know they are in spiritual darkness and so are looking for salvation. Those who think they see have no need of a saviour and will remain in spiritual darkness, because they reject the light of Christ.

Ephesians

2:1   We are all born dead in sin, we have no life and cannot save ourselves.

2:2   The ruler is Satan.

2:3   'All' refers to both Jews and Gentiles. The sinful nature includes our desires (emotions) and our thoughts.

2:4   But with the darkness of God's wrath and punishment for sin comes this great promise of God's rich mercy and love.

5:9   Light brings about the change, it bears fruit (plants need light to grow).

       The fruit is goodness, righteousness and truth and it is this which pleases the Lord.

QUESTIONS

1. How does Jesus expose the darkness of sin, both in the world and in the individual?

2. In Ephesians 5:11 Paul says that the Christian should have nothing to do with the fruitless deeds of darkness? Does this mean we should only have Christian friends? If not, what does it mean?

FOCUS ACTIVITY

A Light in the Darkness.
Allocate group members to equal size teams and give them a picture of a lighthouse to study (see activity diagram on page 60). Give each team a large piece of paper and some pens. Each person has 1 minute, wearing the blindfold, to collectively draw a lighthouse. Extra points are awarded for artistic development, e.g. water, ships, etc. The leader times the 1 minute intervals and tells the team members when to swap over the blindfold, so that the next drawer can continue the picture. At the end hold up the pictures and judge which is best.

Link into the study by pointing out how light (removing the blindfold) exposes mistakes made in the pictures. Jesus claims to be the light of the world, exposing our mistakes individually and in the world.

ACTIVITY

The quiz on page 60 should be done in 2 teams. The winner is the first team to put all 6 rays of yellow light on their light house (see diagram).

Requirements

Each team requires a drawing of a lighthouse pinned onto a board and a set of 8 rays of light , 6 coloured yellow and 2 blue. The rays are randomly numbered from 1-8 on the back and are pinned to the board with the numbers showing. The blue rays introduce an element of luck so that a team member who answers a question incorrectly will not place their team in an irretrievable position.

Rules

A question is put to each team in turn and, if answered correctly, one of the team members chooses a card by calling out its number. The card is turned over and, if yellow, is placed in position on the light house. A blue card is discarded.

If an incorrect answer is given the question is offered to the other team.

Allow 10-15 minutes for the quiz.

Questions

1. How long had the man been blind?

2. Why was the man blind?

3. How did Jesus heal the blind man?

4. What was the name of the pool and what does the name mean?

5. Which day was the man healed?

6. When the Pharisees questioned the man, who did he say Jesus was?

7. Why did the man's parents deny all knowledge of what had happened?

8. The Pharisees said that they were the disciples of whom?

9. What does night/darkness often mean in John's gospel?

10. Why were the Pharisees blind?

11. Who did the Ephesians follow before they became Christians (2:2)?

12. By what have we been saved (Ephesians 2:5)?

13. Name one thing that makes up the fruit of the light (Ephesians 5:9).

14. Name another thing that is part of the fruit of the light.

15. What is your memory verse for today.

16. What is last week's memory verse?

PREPARATION

John 10:1-10

LESSON AIMS

To teach that we can only obtain salvation through Jesus.

The two themes of the gate and the shepherd are inseparably linked in this passage. In this lesson the aim is to concentrate on 'the Gate' and leave the study on the 'Good Shepherd' until next lesson.

10:1 This passage is a continuation from the previous chapter about the healing of the blind man and spiritual blindness (see 10:19-21).

At night the sheep were penned into a stone enclosure with one gap/gate. The shepherd often slept across the entrance to prevent sheep straying or predators entering. The 'unofficial' visitors would be those who would try to get in by the wrong way, because they were up to no good.

10:3 There is no need to interpret the gatekeeper, who is not identified in the parable. The important point here is the relationship between the sheep and the shepherd.

10:4 Eastern shepherds walked in front of their sheep, not behind.

10:6 Note the hearer's inability to understand what Jesus is saying.

10:7 The truth is that Jesus himself is the gate.

10:8 'All who ever came before' cannot possibly mean the prophets in this context, but the false shepherds (religious leaders) of the past and present who were leading the people astray. Jesus is talking here to the Pharisees who are spiritually blind (9:41).

10:9 Again the statement, 'I am the gate'. But now there are two additions, the promises of salvation and sustenance (spiritual).

10:10 The fulness of life is another favourite theme of John. The contrast here is with the self-motivated, self seeking purposes of the false shepherds, and those of the Good Shepherd who wants the abundance of a full life for his sheep.

QUESTIONS

1. In v.9 Jesus says that he is the way of salvation. What about the people who sincerely believe in other religions? Is there any other way to God?

2. How do I discern false teachers from true ones?

Saving Gates. Place two 'gate posts' at one end of the room. Each person has to run between the posts in order to be saved. Designate one person to be the catcher and instruct the remaining group members to hide around the room whilst the catcher is counting to fifty, eyes closed. The catcher has to find the remainig group members and prevent them running through the gate posts. A person hiding is out if the catcher spots them and says their name to prove it, or if the catcher reaches the gate posts before them, touching the gate post to prove it. Have an 'in' bench and an 'out' bench for people to sit when they have come out of hiding, corresponding to whether or not they have been caught.

Link in to the Bible passage by pointing out that there was only one way to safety, i.e. through the gate. Why does Jesus claim that he is the gate to safety?

Photocopy page 63 for each group member.

In this puzzle, the answers to the clues are to be entered in the grid in a clockwise direction around the spiral. Each answer starts from its clue number and the last letter of one answer is the first letter of the following one. Try to answer the clues without reference to the passage.

1. The title Jesus gives himself.
2. Another word for goes in.
3. Those who know Jesus voice.
4. Where the sheep live.
5. What the shepherd calls his sheep by.
6. The quality of life Jesus gives.
7. What the shepherd does for his sheep.
8. The man who enters by the gate.

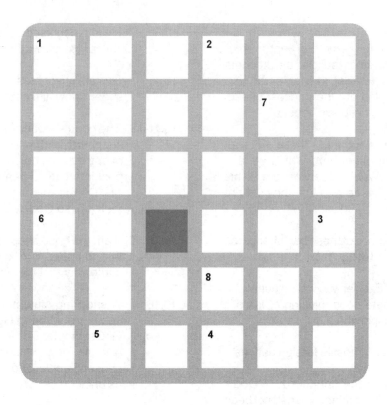

PREPARATION

Ezekiel 34:1-16;
John 10:1-30

LESSON AIMS

To contrast the bad shepherd with the good, and see why Jesus called himself the good shepherd

The passage in John was studied last week and has the twin themes of the Gate and the Shepherd inseparably linked. Concentration on the Shepherd, good v. bad, needs to be emphasised in this week's lesson. The idea of shepherding in Palestine was one easily understood. Although in the 1st Century, shepherds were despised by the affluent and religious people because their anti-social hours meant they were not part of the worshipping community, in the OT Moses was a shepherd, kings were referred to as shepherds (Ezekiel 34:1-4) and God was thought of as a Shepherd (Psalm 23:1).

Ezekiel

34:2   Shepherds of Israel were those responsible for providing leadership, especially the kings, but also the prophets and priests. Ezekiel, in chapter 22, had already singled out the princes, priests and prophets for special rebuke.

34:3   Eat, clothe, slaughter - these were all perks for the shepherd which were a legitimate reward for service, but in this case their offence was that they did not care.

34:4   Further offences of these bad shepherds (cf. Matthew 18:12 - 14).

34:5   Scattered - Ezekiel was writing during the exile and here he is thinking of Israel's exile and dispersion.

34:8   'Wild animals' - hostile foreign nations.

34:10   'I am against the shepherds' - God's judgment of the leaders who had not been true to their calling under God.

34:11   'I myself will search' - the Lord will be the Good Shepherd.

34:12   'from all the places' - Babylon and elsewhere.

These last verses (11-16) can be looked at on one level as prophesying the restoration of the Jews to their land, which was later fulfilled in the time of Nehemiah and Ezra. On another level we see that these verses were perfectly fulfilled in the Lord Jesus Christ, the Good Shepherd.

John

10:2   The good shepherd uses the official gate - he has nothing to hide.

10:3   He is recognised by the watchman and the sheep. He knows them individually by name.

10:4   Eastern shepherds led from the front. These sheep know him as their only true shepherd.

10:11-13 The good shepherd is ready to die, the hired shepherd (bad) will run away at the first sign of any trouble: he doesn't have the sheep's best interests at heart. Cf. Ezekiel 34:1-6, 11-16 - the rulers of Israel were not doing their job, so God said he would take over.

10:14-15 'I am the good shepherd' is repeated. Note that the shepherd knows his sheep in the same way that the Father knows the Son.

10:16   A shocking statement as this implied that Jesus would bring Gentiles into the fold of God's people. To the religious Jew this was a totally new concept. They were God's chosen people, and the Gentile was viewed as unclean.

10:17-18 Christ chose to die for his people in response to God's command. The Father has given Jesus authority to choose. He chose death.

10:19 -21 Where the teachings of Jesus are proclaimed division frequently occurs (cf. 7:43; 9:16).

10:25 Even miracles wouldn't convince the Pharisees of the truth of Jesus' claim.

10:27 Jesus' sheep are those who listen to and follow him. See Mark 8:34-38 for what following Jesus means.

10:28 The assurance of lasting salvation. It cannot be lost.

10:29-30 Both the greatness of God and our eternal security are emphasised here.

1. Contrast in detail the attributes of the bad and the good shepherd.

2. Jesus repeats himself on 2 occasions in the John passage telling his disciples an important fact. What is it?

3. Summarise all the benefits the Good Shepherd brings to his sheep.

Team Challenge. Set up 4 simple relay activities, e.g. running back and forth holding cups of water, wheelbarrow race, hopping race, carrying a book on the head. Divide the group into teams of 5 to race against each other, but for each individual race only 4 team members are allowed to compete, i.e. each team member takes it in turns to sit out. Any team breaking this rule is disqualified.

Link into the Bible study by pointing out that each team member sat out a race for the good of the team. Let's see what Jesus did for us.

Photocopy page 66 for each person.

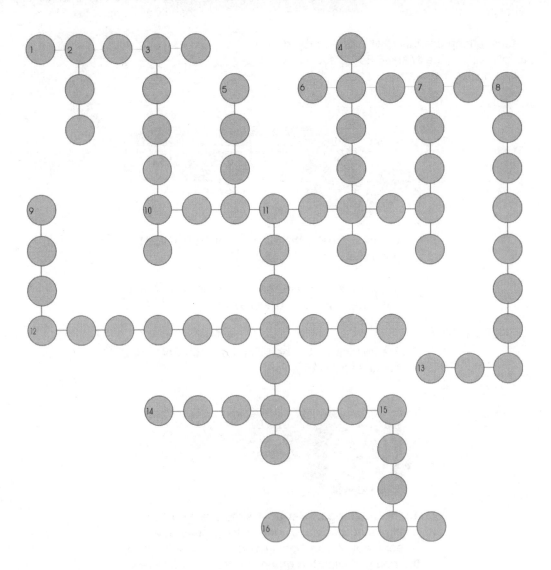

Across

1. The sheep listen to the shepherd's
   _ _ _ _ _ (v.3).
6. What the sheep do to the shepherd (v.4).
10. See 9 down.
12. The name of the feast (v.22).
13. See 16 across.
14. + 15 down. What Jesus gives to his sheep (v.28).
16. + 13 across. Where the sheep live.

Down

2. The number of flocks and shepherds (v.16).
3. The Greek word for Messiah.
4. Who climbs into the sheep pen (v.1)?
5. The shepherd knows his sheep by
   _ _ _ _ (v.3).
7. What the shepherd does for the sheep (v.3).
8. Who opens the gate (v.3)?
9. + 10 across. Who Jesus is (v.11)
11. Where the sheep feed.
15. See 14 across.

PREPARATION

John 11:1-44

LESSON AIMS

To understand that Jesus gives eternal life now, not just when we die.

The Jews of the time had a limited understanding of, and belief in, the resurrection. Jesus, by making this stupendous claim of v.25, is saying it is a person, not a doctrine, who gives life after death and hope now. Doctrine alone cannot bring resurrection and life, only Jesus can.

11:1-3   John is making clear the relationships within the family. The incident referred to in v.2 isn't recorded until later in this gospel (12:1-3). Jesus often visited the family and was very close to the members of it.

11:4   Jesus knew it was God's plan to raise Lazarus - he delays his journey to Bethany so he can better demonstrate the power and glory of God (see v.15).

11:7-8   Bethany is 2 miles from Jerusalem, the source of danger for Jesus.

11:9   The inaccurate time pieces of this period meant that the Jews and Romans divided the day into 2 periods of 12 hours, one of darkness, one of light, with the obvious seasonal variations. Here Jesus is meaning the time of darkness hasn't yet come when he would go to the cross. He is still safe to go to Bethany. Remember that 'darkness' in John's gospel often refers to spiritual darkness (see lesson notes for week 2).

11:11   Lazarus was dead. In no way could this mean that he was only sleeping, as some scholars would have us believe. He had been dead four days - see Martha's reaction (v.39).

11:17   Four days was significant in the contemporary Jewish world. After 4 days it was believed that death was final and that the person's spirit left the tomb. Lazarus was irrevocably dead.

11:20   True to her character, Martha is the first of

the family to go out to meet Jesus.

11:24   Martha has her doctrine right.

11:25   'I am' - a person, not a doctrine. Jesus will raise the dead to life, and will give spiritual life to the soul.

11:32   Mary repeats Martha's statement in v.21.

11:35   The Almighty God lived so intensely as a human he identified with them in the time of death and sorrow.

11:37   They didn't expect him to raise Lazarus, only to have prevented his death.

11:42   The reason for the raising of Lazarus was to reinforce the teaching, to help them believe that Jesus was the Christ.

QUESTIONS

1. It is sometimes said that death is the only certainty in this life. Is this true for Christians?

2. What does it mean to have eternal life (see John 17:3)? Can I experience it now or do I have to wait until I get to heaven?

(Please turn over for activities)

Life-giving Tag. Designate one group member to be the catcher. That person has 'life' and gives it to others by tagging them. As each person is tagged they join the catching team. The game ends once everyone has been caught. Let's look at the Bible to see what Jesus says is the way to get eternal life.

Photocopy page 69 for each person.

With the help of the clues on the right, add one letter to each of the words on the left to make a new word. Place the new letter in the box provided. Then unscramble the letters and write them in the spaces below to give a title Jesus used for himself.

Word		Clue
TUMBLE		What we do in the dark
LOTH		Lazarus' face was wrapped in it
GOD		What God said about creation
MAY		One of Lazarus' sisters
HER		Where we are now
CRETE		God did this in six days
EVE		God's word will last for this long
HAVE		A safe place
RAN		Noah had it for 40 days and 40 nights
DID		Jesus did this so that we can live
SAYS		What Jesus does on hearing Lazarus is ill
ANGER		No need to be afraid of this now
GENTLE		Not Jewish
OX		An animal with a bushy tail
FAR		God is near, have no _ _ _ _
CROWS		What the 24 elders wear in Revelation 4:4
FOR		How many days was Lazarus dead?
AID		Lazarus was _ _ _ _ in the tomb
HEAD		Another word for listened

The _ _ _ _ _ _ _ _ _ _ _ _ _ _ _ the _ _ _ _

PREPARATION

John 13:31 - 14:14

LESSON AIMS

To teach that the believer can be assured of heaven when he/she dies.

This claim of Jesus to be the only way to God is probably the biggest stumbling block to those outside the church. The idea that 'all roads lead to God' is one which pervades current thinking, but it is not the truth. The passage is set in the context of Jesus' forthcoming crucifixion and after Judas has left to betray him (13:30).

13:31-32 The salvation that will result from Jesus' death will bring glory to Jesus and to God himself.

13:33 Jesus is going away, He will be separated from them.

13:34-35 A new command means new in its scope; love for one another should be a characteristic of the believers. Jesus now sets the standard of this love.

13:36 The First Request - 'Where are you going?' This came from Peter and leads into his hasty promises to lay down his life.

13:38 This denial is prophesied in all 4 gospels.

14:1 The disciples no doubt were puzzled and anxious about the event and words of the earlier moments. The answer to anxiety is to trust in God.

14:2 Rooms suggest permanence, a dwelling place.

14:3 Here the reference to Jesus' return is primarily to his second coming.

14:4 They should have known the way. Their subsequent question shows an ignorance for which there was no excuse.

14:5 The Second Request - 'How can we know the way?'

14:6 This is the complete answer to the question. Jesus himself is the way, the true and living way to God (cf. Hebrews 10:19-20). The themes of life and truth which John introduces in the prologue are now expanded in this verse. The person of Jesus is the light and life of John 1:4 and the truth of 1:14. In the early church Christianity was often called 'The Way' (see Acts 9:2; 19:9).

14:7 Again the emphasis here is on the deep inseparable relationship between the Father and the Son. Jesus brought a full revelation of the Father (cf. 1:18).

14:8 The Third Request - 'Show us the Father'.

14:9 After three years they still seemed to be ignorant of the truth of Jesus and his claims.

14:10 Here again the relationship between Father and Son is emphasised to the extent that Jesus' words and works are not human in origin but stem from the Father.

14:11 Belief in God means trusting Jesus. The disciples had all seen God's extraordinary power displayed.

14:12 The greater works are those done in the strength of the Holy Spirit who is to come. The greatest miracle is conversion (see Acts 1:8).

14:13-14 An individual's name summed up his whole person. It is the prayer that Jesus' work will be forwarded which will bring glory to God and Jesus has promised to answer that prayer.

QUESTIONS

1. 'Trust and obey'. Do they always go together? What does it mean to trust God?

2. Will Jesus give us whatever we ask for if we ask for it 'in his name'? What does this mean? How do we reconcile this statement with unanswered prayer, e.g. prayer for healing?

FOCUS ACTIVITY

Water Challenge. Divide the group up into teams of 4-8. Set up a relay race involving carrying water from one station to another. Have a full bowl at the start and an empty bowl at the end. Place various obstacles between the 2 ends, e.g. chairs to climb over, a table to crawl under, objects to run round. Each participant takes a plastic cup containing water, held only between their teeth, and carries it to the finish, where it is emptied into the bowl. That participant has to return to base before the next person goes. The winning team is the one that gets most water into their bowl. Point out at the end that spilling water made getting wet a certainty. Let's look at the Bible to see something else that Jesus said was a certainty (each believer going to heaven).

ACTIVITY

Photocopy page 72 for each person.

Fit the jigsaw pieces into the frame provided to discover today's memory verse. The shaded squares should help you get started.

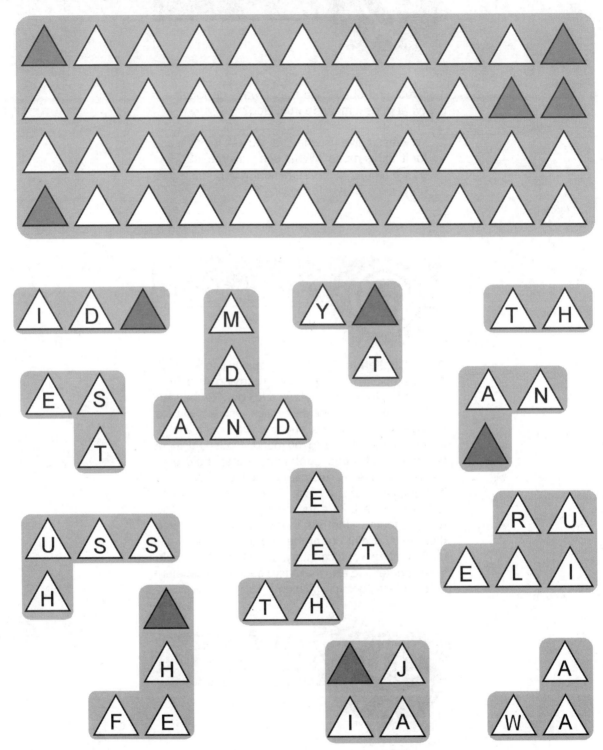

Where does this verse come from?

WEEK 23

The Vine

PREPARATION

John 15:1-17

LESSON AIMS

To teach that the believer's relationship with Jesus is demonstrated by a changed life.

The picture of the vine was often used in the OT to symbolise Israel (cf. Psalm 80:8-10, Isaiah 5:1-7, Jeremiah 2:21). The true vine is Jesus himself, and without him we are and can do nothing. Our very being depends on him.

15:1 'The true vine' points to the fact that Jesus is genuine and not lacking in any way. He's the real Israel (cf. Exodus 4:22). 'My Father' (God) is the gardener or vine dresser, who owns the vineyard and cares for the vines.

15:2 There is no point in keeping branches which do not bear fruit. Pruning is important here, and its purpose is fruitfulness, although at the time it could be painful. (Cf. Hebrews 12:11, Galatians 5:22-23.)

15:3 Jesus points to the importance of his own words, which have achieved the pruning effect on the branches already.

15:5 'I am the vine' - this time the additional phrase is about the branches, or disciples.

15:6 Remain or abide is an important principle. There is no growth, fruit or life without the work of Jesus and the life he gives to the believer.

These branches that are thrown away are probably not the true believers, e.g. Judas. James says 'faith without works is dead' (James 2:17). A true believer must bring forth fruit.

15:7 Those who 'abide' or 'remain' will pray correctly in accordance with the name, character, and will of God.

15:8 The purpose of bearing fruit is to bring glory to God.

15:10 The obedience characterised by Jesus came out of love for the Father (cf. 14:31). So too, the disciples must show their love by obedience to God's commands.

15:11 'My joy .... your joy'. The disciple's joy is dependent on Jesus' joy, which results from self-sacrificial service.

15:12-13 The power of love is demonstrated not only in words but by his death.

15:15 Servants become friends. Friends are able to share; they can share everything. From 16:12-13 we learn that the revelation was still to be completed by the Holy Spirit.

15:16 Normally disciples would choose which Rabbi to follow. This is the reverse; Jesus has chosen them. The initiative is his, as it is in salvation.

Jesus appointed us to bear fruit and then the Father will hear our prayers.

15:16 'In my name' - cf. John 14:13.

QUESTIONS

1. What does it mean to bear fruit?

2. What sort of discipline do you think Christians suffer?

3. What are the results of no discipline?

(Please turn over for activities)

Changing Lives. Give each person a piece of paper and a pen and ask them a series of questions (see below). The answer to each question is written at the top of the paper, then folded over to hide the writing and passed to the person on their left, ready for the next question. At the end of the questions the papers are unfolded and the resulting scenarios read out to the group.

Introduce the activity by telling the group that they are writing a 'soap opera' storyline, or blockbuster romance, about two people whose lives were changed when they met. Ask them to write down the following:

1. The name of the hero (could be real or fictional).
2. The name of the heroine.
3. Where did they meet?
4. What did he say to her?
5. What did she say to him?
6. What happened?

Link into the Bible passage by pointing out that the stories were about two people who had their lives changed as a result of meeting. Let's see what Jesus had to say about the way our lives should change as a result of knowing him.

Photocopy page 75 for each person.

When the letters in each column are correctly positioned in the boxes above them, you will discover a verse from John 15. One letter has been placed to help you on your way.

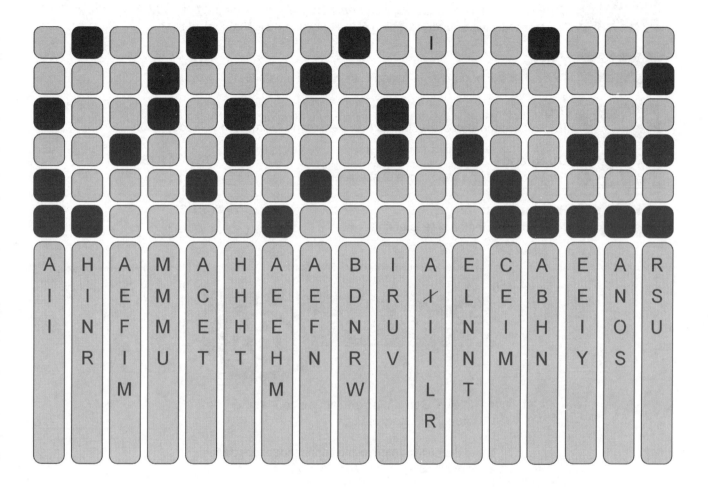

Which verse is the statement from?

OVERVIEW
Ruth - the Bridge from Chaos to Splendour

Week 24 | **Chaos**   *Genesis 19:30-38, Numbers 25:1-3, Deuteronomy 2:1-9, Judges 2:11-20; 3:12-14*
To come to a clearer understanding of the background to the book of Ruth.

Week 25 | **Trust**   *Ruth 1:1-22*
To teach the importance of trusting God in all circumstances.

Week 26 | **Provision**   *Ruth 2:1-23*
To introduce the idea of the kinsman-redeemer and the meaning of redemption.

Week 27 | **Obedience**   *Ruth 3:1-18*
To demonstrate the importance of obedience.

Week 28 | **Redemption**   *Ruth 4:1-22*
To develop the theme of redemption.

SERIES AIMS

1. To see God's plan of redemption worked out through the story of Ruth.

2. To understand more of the importance of obedience in our lives.

MEMORY WORK

May you be richly rewarded by the LORD,
the God of Israel, under whose wings
you have come to take refuge.

Ruth 2:12

Ruth - the Bridge from Chaos to Splendour

The book of Ruth is part of the historical section of the Old Testament and is set in a period of transition from the chaos of the Judges to the splendour of the reign of David. The story takes place during the last years of the Judges (Ruth 1:1; 4:13-17) when 'everyone did as he saw fit' (Judges 21:25). It is a story about a Moabite girl, a foreigner, who turns to Israel's God and becomes part of his people, and in so doing is blessed. Her son becomes the grandfather of Israel's great king, David, which is remarkable considering the history of Moab.

The time of the Judges and the history of Moab will be studied in detail in the first week of this series. It was a period in Israel's history of moral and religious decadence and there was enmity between Israel and Moab. The story starts during a time of famine when an Israelite family decided to move to Moab in search of food. There the husband, Elimelech, died, his 2 sons married Moabite women and, 10 years after arrival in Moab, both sons died. The wife, Naomi, heard that food was plentiful in Canaan and planned to return there. One of her daughters-in-law, Ruth, went with her. Ruth showed by her declaration of faith (1:16-17) and her selfless devotion to Naomi (2:11) that she had embraced the faith of the living God. On their return, desolate and poor, their plight was noted by Boaz, a near relative, who eventually acted the part of the kinsman-redeemer by buying back their land and marrying Ruth.

The theme of the book is redemption. Boaz foreshadows Christ - he comes from Bethlehem, he is able to redeem, he is under no obligation to redeem, he decides to redeem by grace and the redemption is costly. Ruth foreshadows us - a total outsider, (pagan, a woman and a widow), who is brought into the centre of God's plan. Her part in the story is one of obedience to her mother-in-law.

In the second week of the series we discover the need to trust God in **all** circumstances. Elimelech's family did not trust God in a time of hardship, so left the Promised Land. This is contrasted with Ruth's willingness to return to Canaan with Naomi, even though they had no means of support. The concept of redemption, clearly demonstrated by the acts of Boaz, is developed in the third and fifth weeks of the series, and the importance of obedience is studied in the fourth.

Throughout the story of Ruth we see God's love joining with man's actions to accomplish the transition from chaos to splendour.

PREPARATION

Genesis 19:30-38,
Numbers 25:1-3,
Deuteronomy 2:1-9,
Judges 2:11-20; 3:12-
14

LESSON AIMS

To come to a clearer understanding of the background to the book of Ruth.

Genesis

This is an unsavoury story and the teacher must decide how much detail to include in the light of the maturity of the group being taught.

19:30   Zoar, along with Sodom and Gomorrah, was one of the cities of the plain and was situated south of the Dead Sea.

19:37   Moab was the son of Lot by his eldest daughter. The name sounds like the Hebrew for 'from father' and was given to both his descendants and the land where they lived. The centre of the area was plateau land to the east of the Dead Sea north of Edom. The plateau land was bisected by the River Arnon and already had an established population. The descendants of Lot intermarried with these and eventually became the dominant group. After a period of war with the kings from the East (Genesis 14:5), Moab emerged as an organised kingdom with good buildings, strong defences, established farming patterns, pottery, etc. as shown by modern archaeological evidence.

Deuteronomy

2:1   This happened following the Israelites rebellion against God when the spies reported on the problems that would be encountered if they entered the Promised Land (1:19-46).

2:2   There is a gap of many years between v.1 and v.2 (see v.7).

2:8   See map on page 80.

2:9   God commands the Israelites not to provoke Moab. The Moabites refused Israel's request for passage along the main north-south road known as the King's Highway (Judges 11:14:18), causing the Israelites to make a detour.

Numbers

Prior to this Balak, king of Moab, asked the prophet, Balaam, to put a curse on the Israelites because the Moabites were afraid of them (Numbers 22:1-6).

25:1-2   These verses demonstrate the evil practices of the Moabites.

Judges

The period of the Judges was characterised by a merry-go-round of disobedience, apostasy, foreign intervention, cries for help, deliverance and the patience of a long-suffering God. This 'dark' time in Israel's history was even more remarkable considering it followed on from the great acts of God in bringing the Children of Israel into the Promised Land under the guidance of Joshua. Often periods of defeat follow times of great victory.

2:13   The Baals were pagan deities worshipped by the Canaanites. The main one, referred to as Baal (without any suffix), was Hadad, the storm-god. Ashtaroth was one of Baal's consorts and was a fertility goddess.

2:16   The judges were not just arbiters between the people but were also the civil and military leaders. The choice of the judge was in God's hands; there was no dynastic succession.

3:13   The City of Palms was Jericho.

With this in mind it is incredible that Ruth, a Moabitess, would not only be the great-grandmother of David but would also be in the ancestral line of Jesus (Matthew 1:1,5). Her life and place in the Biblical records points out that 'obedience which comes from faith' (Romans 1:5) was an important factor.

QUESTIONS

1. List the things that were wrong in Israel during the time of the Judges. What similarities can be found with a) our present culture and b) the church?

2. Can you think of other instances in the Bible where defeat follows great victory? (If you need help, look up Joshua 6:27 - 7:9, 1 Samuel 10 - 11).

   What can we learn from this?

FOCUS ACTIVITY

What Makes a Blockbuster? Ask the group to make a list of the key ingredients in a good film, e.g. gore, action, romance. Discuss why they have listed the items. Link into Judges containing all these ingredients.

VISUAL AID

Map - see page 80

ACTIVITY

Photocopy page 81 for each person.

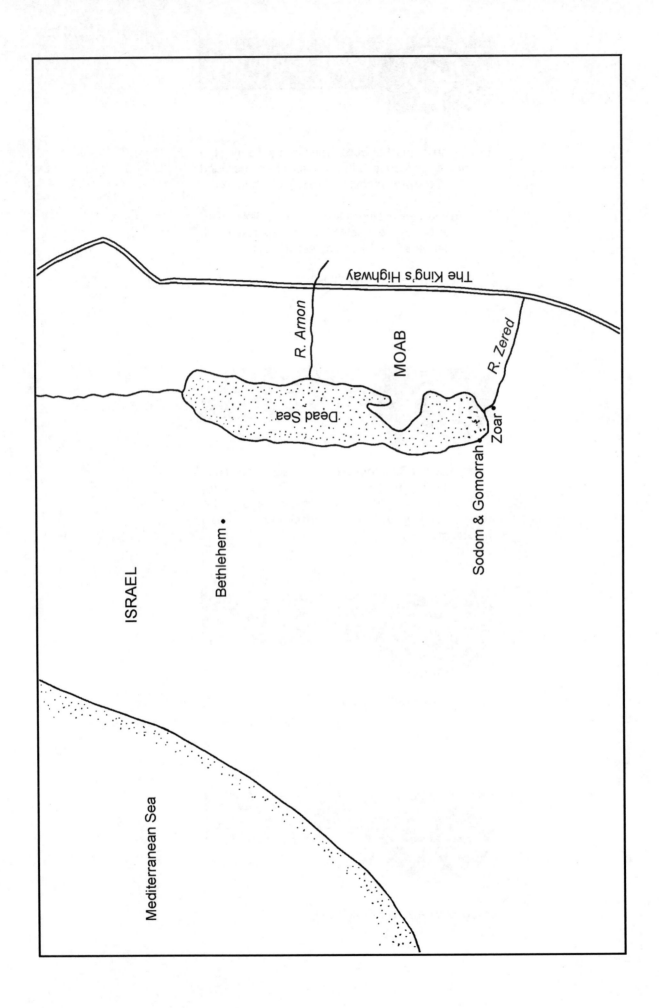

The Word square contains 12 words connected with the story of Ruth. Each word reads in a straight line horizontally, vertically or diagonally. No letter is used more than once.

N	O	R	E	F	U	G	E	M	R	BETHLEHEM
A	E	B	V	S	E	E	E	R	E	BOAZ
M	B	Y	E	C	O	H	O	N	W	CHAOS
S	E	O	A	D	E	A	R	D	A	COSTLY
N	I	R	A	L	I	U	H	D	R	FAMINE
I	G	A	H	Z	T	E	S	C	D	GRACE
K	H	T	E	H	S	A	N	W	E	KINSMAN
F	E	Y	L	T	S	O	C	C	D	OBEDIENCE
B	I	F	A	M	I	N	E	T	E	REDEMPTION
N	O	I	T	P	M	E	D	E	R	REFUGE
										REWARDED
										RUTH

Now, starting from the top and reading from left to right, write down the remaining letters to discover the what was happening in Israel at that time in their history.

WEEK 25
Trident Trust

PREPARATION
Ruth 1:1-22

LESSON AIMS
To teach the importance of trusting God in all circumstances.

Ruth

1:1 The judges were the leaders of Israel prior to the kings (see lesson notes for week 24, Judges 2:16). Their period extended from c.1380-1050 B.C. and it was a time of frequent apostasy (Judges 2:16-19).

The famine is not recorded in the book of Judges.

Bethlehem means 'house of food' and was to become the home-town of David.

The family not only left the Promised Land, which indicated their lack of trust in God, but also went to the land of their enemy. Moab was a land of idolaters with a way of life opposed to the worship of God. The journey from Bethlehem was approximately 50 miles.

1:2 Elimelech means 'God is king'.
Naomi means 'pleasant'.
Mahlon means 'weakly'.
Kilion means 'pining'.

1:3 The death of a husband would be a real blow because being a widow meant being vulnerable.

1:4 The sons married Moabite women. Although the Israelites were warned not to marry into the tribes of Canaan (Deuteronomy 7:1-6), marriage with the Moabites was not specifically forbidden. However, Deuteronomy 23:3 states that no male Moabite or his sons is to be allowed to enter the assembly of the Lord even down to the tenth generation. It seems that marriage with female proselytes was allowed, e.g. Salmon with Rahab (Matthew 1:5).

1:5 Both sons died, leaving Naomi without protection or provision for her needs.

1:6 Naomi is still being swayed by circumstances.

1:11 It was the custom for a childless widow to be married to her late husband's younger brother (Deuteronomy 25:5-10).

1:14 Orpah returns to Moab but Ruth opts to continue with Naomi.

1:16-17 A declaration of Ruth's faith. She had come to trust in the true God **despite** her circumstances. Note the similarity with modern marriage vows.

1:20-21 Marah means 'bitter'. Naomi had left Bethlehem with a husband and 2 sons but returns with nothing. Her fullness has been turned into emptiness. Note that she puts her misfortunes down to God.

1:22 'Ruth, the Moabitess,' is a reminder of Ruth's foreign origins.

The barley harvest began in April, followed a few weeks later by the wheat harvest.

QUESTIONS

1. How should we react in adverse circumstances? What do you do at school when friends laugh at you for being a Christian?

2. How can we see God's over-ruling in this passage?

82

Whom do you trust? Ask for a volunteer who trusts you. Bring out a blindfold and a tub of worms (either dug out of the garden or bought as bait from a fishing shop). Take the lid off the tub of worms and stir. Blindfold the volunteer and ask them to open their mouth. Do they trust you not to feed them worms? Place a spoonful of cold cooked spaghetti in the volunteer's mouth and see what happens. Whatever the reaction, use it to lead into the importance of knowing whom to trust. Let's see who in today's Bible passage trusted God and how they demonstrated that trust.

Photocopy page 84 for each person.

Unscramble each row of letters to make a five-lettered word. Having done that, enter them in the grid in such a way that the central column, reading downwards, spells a commodity that was in short supply.

SLEBS

BLEER

AUDJH

GLSRI

AGTNR

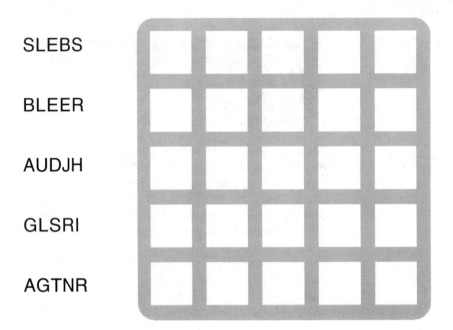

PREPARATION

Ruth 2:1-23

LESSON AIMS

To introduce the idea of the kinsman-redeemer and the meaning of redemption.

Boaz was a middle-aged, well-to-do Israelite man with a secure social standing. Ruth, by contrast, was a young, poor, foreign woman, and a widow, so would have had little status in Israelite society.

2:1   Boaz is mentioned in both of Jesus' genealogies (Matthew 1:5, Luke 3:32).

2:2   Ruth, as a young, foreign woman, would be very vulnerable out alone in the fields, but she is keen to provide for Naomi. The Mosaic law ordered landowners to leave what the harvesters missed for the poor, aliens, widows and fatherless (Leviticus 19:9-10, Deuteronomy 24:19).

2:3   'As it turned out' - God's providence is at work.

2:4   These greetings suggest that Boaz is a kindly, God-fearing man whom the harvesters respected. (Israelites were very careful not to break the third commandment.)

2:6   The Moabitess - the foreigner.

2:11   Ruth's selflessness has not gone unnoticed.

2:12   'Under whose wings' gives a picture of a bird protecting its young (cf. Psalm 91:4).

2:14-15 Boaz makes sure Ruth has enough to eat with some to spare for Naomi (see v.17-18). He has already started to provide for her needs of food and protection (see v. 8-9).

2:17   Gleaning involved picking up remnants of grain left by the harvesters. An ephah was about 22 litres, so was a lot of grain to get from gleaning! This was obtained through Boaz' generosity.

2:20   Naomi recognises that Boaz is a kinsman-redeemer and encourages Ruth to stay close to him (v.22). The kinsman-redeemer was responsible for protecting the interests of needy members of his family, for buying back (redeeming) land that a poor relative had needed to sell, for avenging the killing of a family member and for redeeming a relative sold into slavery (see Leviticus 25:23-28,47-49). As well as redeeming the land, the closest relative also had the opportunity to marry the widow, although only the brother-in-law was obliged to do so (Deuteronomy 25:5-10).

2:23   Barley and wheat harvests would have covered a time span of several weeks.

QUESTIONS

1. How does what we have learnt about the kinsman-redeemer prefigure the redemptive work of Jesus?

2. From what have we been redeemed? In what way does this help in daily life at home and at school?

(Please turn over for activities)

FOCUS ACTIVITY

Divide the group into teams. Each team needs a bucket and 5 table tennis balls or balls of scrunched up newspaper. Place the buckets in a row and mark a line sufficiently far from the buckets to cause difficulty when trying to throw the balls into the buckets. Give each team member 3 counters. The teams line up behind the line and the team members take it in turns to throw the 5 balls into the bucket. Each time they miss they forfeit a counter. If they miss the bucket once all their counters are gone they are consigned to gaol. A person can be redeemed by one of their team mates who has not yet thrown their balls giving up one of their counters. The winning team is the one with most members at the end of the contest.

Use the activity to explain the meaning of 'redemption' to the group.

ACTIVITY

Photocopy page 87 for each person.

In this spiral the answers to the clues are entered in a clockwise direction. Each answer starts from its clue number and the last letter from one answer is the first letter of the following one. You will need to look up the verses in your Bible for some of the questions.

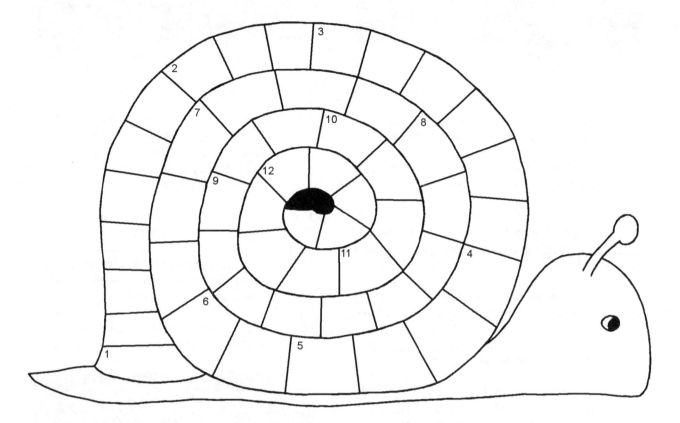

1. How Naomi addressed Ruth (v.2).

2. Orpah's sister-in-law?

3. What season of the farming year was it?

4. How Boaz heard of Ruth's deeds (v.11).

5. What Boaz told Ruth to do (v. 14).

6. Boaz's instructions to his workers (v.16).

7. Further instructions from Boaz (v.16)!

8. Naomi's husband.

9. Ruth was protected from what (v.22)?

10. Ruth's country of birth.

11. What Ruth ate (v.14).

12. The famous king in Boaz's family (4:22).

PREPARATION

Ruth 3:1-18

LESSON AIMS

To demonstrate the importance of obedience.

3:1   Marriages were arranged by parents, so it was right for Naomi to take the initiative.

3:2   As Boaz is a kinsman-redeemer Naomi had the sanction of the law behind her.

    Once the grain was harvested winnowing took place. During this time the men took it in turns to sleep on the threshing floor to guard the grain.

3:3-4   Naomi gave Ruth what could seem to be very 'forward' instructions to prepare herself like a bride. Women were not normally present during the evening party. Ruth's integrity was not in question (see v. 11).

    NB Naomi had the law on her side (Deuteronomy 25:5-10) and she did not press the law for herself, as she was entitled to do. Boaz was already supplying Ruth's needs of food and protection (2:8-9,15-16).

    By uncovering his feet Ruth was not being immoral, i.e. she did not lie at his side but made sure that she disturbed him.

3:5-6   Ruth obeyed her mother-in-law's instructions.

3:9   'Spreading the garment over' symbolised marriage (cf. Ezekiel 16:8).

3:10   Boaz was Naomi's generation, not Ruth's.

3:11   Ruth's integrity is upheld.

3:12   Boaz was concerned to do the right thing. How Boaz was related to Ruth's former husband is unknown, but the nearest male relative had the first option to redeem the field and marry the widow. Boaz had already shown himself willing to be Ruth's protector but he did not want to bypass the law which gave priority to another.

3:13   'As surely as the **LORD** lives' - Boaz commits himself by oath to do the right thing.

3:14   Boaz sent Ruth home before anyone else was about to avoid prying eyes and gossip and so protect her reputation.

3:16-17   Ruth goes home with 6 measures of barley and Naomi's emptiness is turned to fullness.

QUESTIONS

1. Ruth was obedient to Naomi. Who are we commanded to obey? (Look up John 14:15, Ephesians 6:1, Romans 13:1.)

2. Why is obedience important?

3. How did Ruth's obedience assist the working out of God's plan?

The Deadly Chocolate. Prior to the session buy a variety box of individually wrapped chocolates. Choose one variety of chocolate and remove all but one of those chocolates. Take the remaining chocolate, open it carefully and stick some pins through the middle of the chocolate so that they are hidden. Rewrap the chocolate and replace it in the box. Remove sufficient remaining chocolates to leave the same number of chocolates in the box as people in the group. Introduce the morning as starting with a treat. Tell the group that they can each choose a chocolate but they are not to open them until told to do so. Hand the chocolates round. Ask the person who has chosen the doctored chocolate to give it back to you. Everyone else can eat their chocolate. Deal with any comments regarding being unfair, etc. Open the doctored chocolate and break it in half to show the pins. Point out the importance of obedience. Give the person who chose the doctored chocolate a replacement.

Let's look at the Bible to see what happened when Ruth was ordered to do something.

The quiz on page 90 should be done in 2 teams. The winner is the first team to collect 7 letter cards and rearrange them into a word. A letter card is obtained by answering a question correctly.

Requirements

A set of 8 letter cards for each team. Each set has 7 cards with a letter and 1 blank.
Team A's cards read K I N S M A N,
team B's read R E D EE M E R
The backs of the cards are numbered randomly from 1-8 to make it easy to indicate which card is being chosen. The 2 blank cards are included to allow for an element of luck so that anyone answering a question incorrectly will not place their team in an irretrievable position.

Rules

Each set of cards is placed numbered side up on a table or board.

A question is put to each team in turn and, if answered correctly, one of the team members chooses a card by calling out its number. The card is turned over so that both teams can see it. If the card is blank it is discarded.

If an incorrect answer is given the question is put to the other team.

Allow 10-15 minutes for the quiz.

Quiz Questions

1. In which period of Israel's history did the story of Ruth take place?

2. How does the Bible tell us people generally behaved at that period in Israel's history?

3. Name Ruth's parents-in-law.

4. Name their children.

5. Why did the family leave Israel?

6. What sad thing happened in Moab?

7. Why did Naomi want to return to Israel?

8. What does Bethlehem mean?

9. What did Ruth do in order to get food?

10. What had Boaz heard about Ruth?

11. What did Boaz tell Ruth to do?

12. What did Naomi tell Ruth to do at the end of barley harvest?

13. Why was it right for Ruth to do what Naomi said? (What relationship was Boaz to Naomi?)

14. What does 'redeem' mean?

15. What did Boaz tell Ruth he would do?

16. What did Boaz give Ruth to take back to Naomi?

PREPARATION

Ruth 4:1-22

4:1   The town gate was the normal place for business deals and legal transactions.

4:2   The town council - a full legal court.

4:3   Boaz is reminding the kinsman that he must redeem or buy the land that Naomi (or Elimelech) would have to sell (or had sold).

4:5   The other part of the bargain is to marry Ruth.

4:6   Taking another wife could be very costly and could endanger the estate. The first born son of the new wife took the name of her first husband and inherited his land. Any other sons born to that marriage were included with the rest of the second husband's sons as heirs of his estate. When he died his first born son got twice the portion of the other sons (i.e. the estate was split between them). Boaz was prepared to pay the price. This highlights Boaz's generosity and kindness to the 2 widows.

4:7-8   Handing over the sandal was a symbolic ceremony to show that the right of possession had passed from one person to another (cf. Joshua 1:3).

4:9   Public witnesses were needed to attest all legal dealings.

4:12   The story of Judah and Tamar (Genesis 38:1-30), although unsavoury, referred to levirate marriage (Deuteronomy 25:5-10). Tamar had been tacitly refused by Judah, but Boaz had honoured his obligation to Ruth. Perez, who was born to Tamar as a result of her trick, was an ancestor of Boaz, so there was local interest in the story.

4:15   'Better to you than 7 sons'. Seven was considered the perfect number and sons were a sign of God's blessing, so Ruth's selflessness gave Naomi very great joy.

LESSON AIMS

To develop the theme of redemption.

Summary: **Boaz** - came from Bethlehem; was obedient to the law; was able to redeem; was under no obligation to redeem; chose to redeem by grace; knew redemption would be costly. **Ruth** - a total outsider (pagan, woman, widow) brought into the centre of God's plan (4:13-17).

QUESTIONS

1. How does the summary point forward to the redemptive work of Jesus?

2. What was Ruth's role in the story?

3. How was her obedience rewarded?

FOCUS ACTIVITY

On Trial Form the group into a jury. Present three crimes. Each time ask the jury to state whether or not the person is guilty. A leader acts as the judge and passes sentence on the guilty parties. Another leader then steps forward and offers to take the punishment. (You might want to have a specific punishment, e.g. a custard pie in the face.) Discuss what happened to the guilty parties. What did they deserve? What did they get? Let's look at the Bible to see what happened to Ruth and what that teaches us about the way God deals with us.

ACTIVITY

This passage is good for acting out. The group is split in half and asked to prepare a play from the passage to act to each other. It can be the Bible story or a modern adaptation. Each group is responsible for organising themselves. They should appoint a director, who will decide with the group on the script and apportion parts.

Bible Timeline

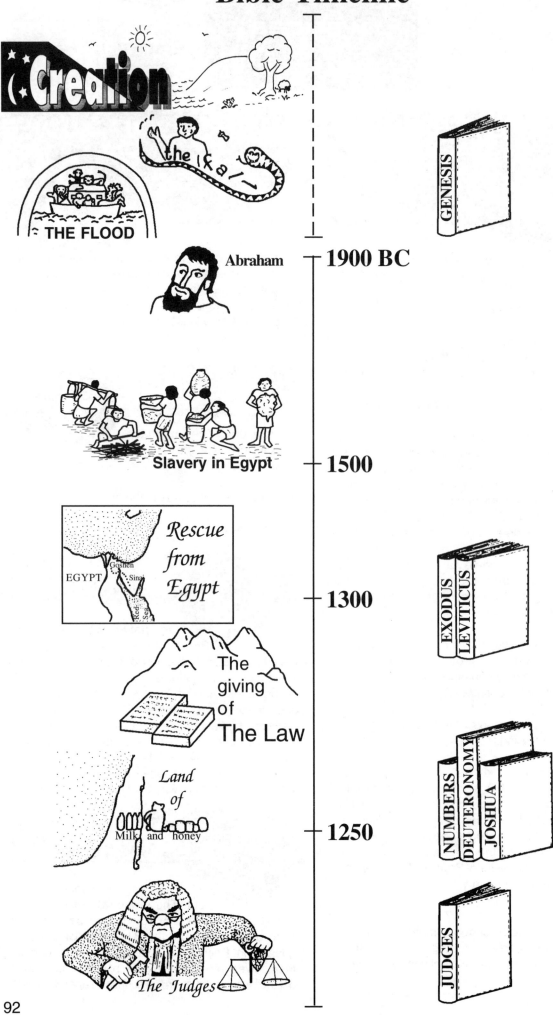

Creation

THE FLOOD

Abraham

Slavery in Egypt

Rescue from Egypt

EGYPT — Goshen · Sinai · Red Sea

The giving of The Law

Land of Milk and honey

The Judges

1900 BC

1500

1300

1250

GENESIS

EXODUS LEVITICUS

NUMBERS DEUTERONOMY JOSHUA

JUDGES

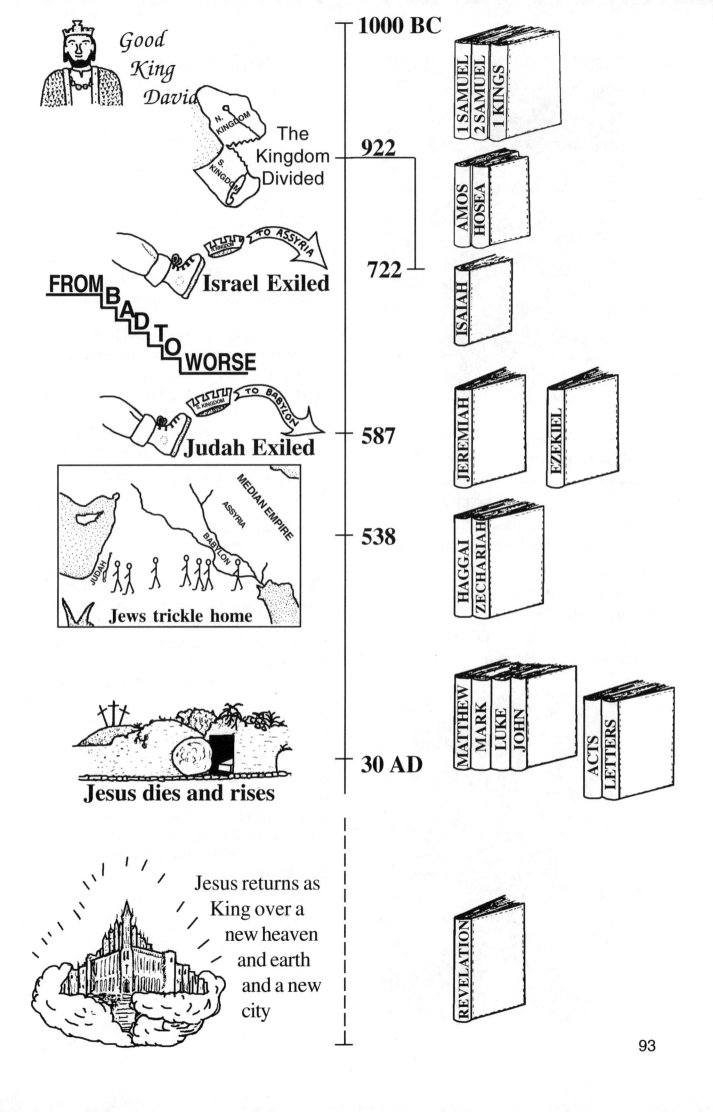

Good King David

The Kingdom Divided

FROM BAD TO WORSE

Israel Exiled

Judah Exiled

Jews trickle home

Jesus dies and rises

Jesus returns as King over a new heaven and earth and a new city

1000 BC

922

722

587

538

30 AD

1 SAMUEL 2 SAMUEL 1 KINGS

AMOS HOSEA

ISAIAH

JEREMIAH EZEKIEL

HAGGAI ZECHARIAH

MATTHEW MARK LUKE JOHN ACTS LETTERS

REVELATION

The Game is Up
OLD TESTAMENT

Book 1: Genesis, Exodus, Numbers, Joshua
Book 2: Judges, Ruth, 1&2 Samuel, 1 & 2 Kings, 2 Chronicles, Nehemiah, Esther, Job, Jeremiah, Daniel, Jonah. Judges, Ruth, 1&2 Samuel, 1& 2 Kings, 2 Chronicles; Nehemiah, Esther, Job, Jeremiah, Daniel, Jonah.

Take the Bible seriously
and have loads of fun while you are at it!

Are you looking to add another dimension to your teaching? Do you want to encourage your children to read the Bible? Do you want them to have strong Biblical foundations without compromising on fun and activity? TnT have developed The Game Is Up for this very purpose. There is a companion volume to this book: The Game is Up Old Testament Book 1 which covers Genesis, Exodus, Numbers and Joshua. There are also plans for books on the New Testament to come out in the following year.

☺ The successful On the Way series continued with extra games and activities.
☺ Book 1: 80 game selections;
☺ Book 2: 96 game selections
☺ Flexible enough to be used with any curriculum
☺ Strong Biblical Emphasis
☺ Multi age (3-11s)
☺ Ideal for Holiday Bible Club; Vacation Bible School

All the games are directly linked to the lessons with strong Biblical emphasis that covers all major Christian doctrines. Visual aids for photocopying and clearly explained teaching points make this an excellent addition to any church resource library.
Book One covers Genesis, Exodus, Numbers and Joshua.
Book 2 covers Judges, Ruth, 1&2 Samuel, 1 & 2 Kings, 2 Chronicles, Nehemiah, Esther, Job, Jeremiah, Daniel, Jonah. Judges, Ruth, 1&2 Samuel, 1& 2 Kings, 2 Chronicles; Nehemiah, Esther, Job, Jeremiah, Daniel, Jonah.

The On The Way series continues
Look out for Book 2

Rescue (Easter)
Paul (Acts 9-16 and 17-18)
Philippians
1 Thessalonians
Suffering

Syllabus for On The Way for 11-14s

Book 1 (28 weeks)	Book 3 (28 weeks)	Book 5 (26 weeks)
Abraham (7) Jacob (7) The Messiah (Christmas) (2) Jesus said, 'I am ...' (7) Ruth (5)	Joseph (7) People in Prayer (7) The Saviour of the World (Christmas)(3) Is God Fair? (Predestination) (2) Learning from a Sermon (3) The Sermon on the Mount (6)	Bible Overview (26)
Book 2 (25 weeks)	**Book 4 (25 weeks)**	**Book 6 (27 weeks)**
Rescue (Easter) (3) Paul (Acts 9-16) (7) Philippians (5) Paul (Acts 17-18) (3) 1 Thessalonians (6) Suffering (1)	Psalms (Easter) (2) Paul's Latter Ministry (7) Colossians (5) Choose Life (Hell & Judgment) (2) The Kings (9)	A Selection of Psalms (5) The Normal Christian Life (7) Revelation (9) Homosexuality (1) The Dark Days of the Judges (5)

The books can be used in any order.

The number in brackets indicates the number of lessons in a series.

For more information about *On the Way for 11-14s* please contact:
Christian Focus Publications, Fearn, Tain, Ross-shire, IV20 1TW / Tel: +44 (0) 1862 871 011 or
TnT Ministries, 29 Buxton Gardens, Acton, London, W3 9LE / Tel: +44 (0) 20 8992 0450

Christian Focus Publications publishes biblically-accurate books for adults and children. If you are looking for quality Bible teaching for children then we have a wide and excellent range of Bible story books - from board books to teenage fiction, we have it covered. You can also try TnT's complete teaching Syllabus for 3-9 year olds; 9-11 year olds as well as the pre-school age group. These children's books are bright, fun and full of biblical truth, an ideal way to help children discover Jesus Christ for themselves. Our aim is to help children find out about God and get them enthusiastic about reading the Bible, now and later in their lives. Find us at our web page: www.christianfocus.com

 TnT Ministries

TnT Ministries (which stands for Teaching and Training) was launched in February 1993 by Christians from a broad variety of denominational backgrounds who were concerned that teaching the Bible to children be taken seriously. The leaders were in charge of the Sunday School of 50 teachers at St Helen's Bishopsgate, an evangelical church in the City of London, for 13 years, during which time a range of Biblical teaching materials was developed. TnT Ministries also runs training days for Sunday School teachers.